Chronicles
of
Corporate
Change

———

Chronicles
of
Corporate
Change

---

*Management Lessons from
AT&T and Its Offspring*

Leonard A. Schlesinger, Davis Dyer,
Thomas N. Clough, AND Diane Landau

Lexington Books

D.C. Heath and Company/Lexington, Massachusetts/Toronto

Note: Case material of the Harvard Graduate School of Business Administration is prepared as the basis for class discussion rather than to illustrate either effective or ineffective handling of an administrative solution.

Library of Congress Cataloging-in-Publication Data

Chronicles of corporate change.

Includes index.
1. American Telephone and Telegraph Company—Reorganization.   2. Northwestern Bell Telephone Company.   3. Telephone—United States.   4. Telecommunication—United States.   5. Organizational effectiveness.   I. Schlesinger, Leonard A.
II. American Telephone and Telegraph Company.
HE8846.A55C47 1987   384.6'065'73   86-45555
ISBN 0-669-13685-9 (alk. paper)

Published simultaneously in Canada
Printed in the United States of America
Casebound International Standard Book Number: 0-669-13685-9
Library of Congress Catalog Card Number: 86-45555

The paper used in this publication meets the minimum requirements of American National Standard for Information Sciences—Permanance of Paper for Printed Library Materials, ANSI Z39.48-1984.

87 88 89 90 8 7 6 5 4 3 2 1

Contents

Figures and Tables

Figures

Tables

Preface

This book tells the inside, human and managerial, story of a company coping with dramatic upheaval. Through personal testimony and industry analysis, it focuses on the changes that AT&T and one of its operating companies, Northwestern Bell,[a] passed through in their halting move from a regulated to a competitive environment over a fifteen-year period. The book offers lessons and guidelines for managers seeking to understand how organizations adapt and change over time, particularly in response to regulatory, technological, and competitive pressures.

Deregulation of telecommunications is occurring worldwide. In 1985 Japan and Britain liberalized their government-controlled telecommunications monopolies. West Germany may not be far behind. The German government, struggling with the costs of a Post Ministry that relies on a huge bureaucracy built on a maze of regulations dating from the 1920s, is aware that technologies have dramatically changed and that the traditional way of doing things brings high costs in both domestic and international markets.

Deregulation has also spread to other U.S. industries, such as financial services, airlines, trucking, and energy. It has been suggested that the United States deregulate its postal service in the quest for greater efficiency and innovation. How should such organizations be restructured? How can managers and employees learn to be responsive to changed circumstances and new expectations? How will their working environments differ? What are the

---

[a]As of January 1, 1984, Northwestern Bell became a part of U S WEST, Inc., one of the seven regional holding companies created by the AT&T divestiture (see chapter 10).

problems involved in redesigning organizations and retraining personnel to compete? How feasible are such changes and what are
their costs?

From the early 1970s to the mid-1980s, AT&T scrambled to
succeed amid changing rules. Shifting public policies periodically
forced the company to redesign its strategy, reorganize its structure,
and reorient its employees. AT&T's difficulties in responding and
adapting to deregulation were complicated by its need to transform
an entrenched management culture that had long supported
AT&T's traditional mandate under regulation: providing universal,
high-quality, low-cost telephone service. Though unmatched in
scale and drama, the saga of the Bell System's breakup and its leaders' efforts to manage the process of change illustrates problems and
solutions generally applicable to companies now confronting new
levels of competitive rivalry both domestically and internationally.

We have arranged the material in this book to be read in either
of two ways. From cover to cover, the narrative tells the entire story
of the Bell System's move from a regulated to a deregulated environment. Along the way, however, we've sectioned the text so that
readers interested in particular parts of the story can follow those
subplots independently.

Part I traces the rise of AT&T to its position as a regulated
monopoly and describes the first glimmerings of fundamental
changes coming in the 1970s. Part II carries the story through the
end of the 1970s, focusing on the efforts of AT&T and Northwestern Bell to adapt to deregulation and mounting competitive rivalry.
Part III covers the period from 1980 to 1982 when AT&T and
Northwestern Bell struggled to cope with increasing competition
amid an extremely uncertain policy environment. Part IV deals with
the response of AT&T and U S West (the new regional holding company that owns Northwestern Bell) to the divestiture.

The origin of this book lies in a series of cases developed under the
direction of Leonard A. Schlesinger at the Harvard Business School
in the late 1970s. First used in a second-year M.B.A. course entitled
"Designing Complex Organizations," the cases eventually migrated
to the final week of the organizational behavior course taught in

the first year of the MBA program.[1] Focusing on reorganizations at AT&T and Northwestern Bell in 1974 and 1978, the cases provided a climactic conclusion to the course. Although the management issues and dilemmas posed at AT&T unfolded on a grand, unprecedented scale, the cases nonetheless brought together most of the elements taught in the course: the relationship between strategy and structure; the relationship between organization and environment; problems of staffing and motivating employees to face new challenges.

After the Federal Communications Commission (FCC) restructured competition in the telecommunications industry in 1980 with its Computer Inquiry II, two more cases were written to describe AT&T's and Northwestern Bell's plans for compliance. Shortly after these cases were completed, public policy again wrought a dramatic change in the story, this time through the divestiture agreement of 1982. Once again two new cases were prepared.[2] By the end of 1985, then, the series consisted of nine cases describing the transformation of AT&T from the breakdown of its traditional regulation to the breakup of the Bell System. Together, the nine cases chronicle a saga that is both intrinsically dramatic and full of important managerial lessons about organizational change and adaptation.

We recount the history of this material for a reason. Cases written over a long period and by many hands inevitably betray differences of style and emphasis. In editing them for this book, we've tried to smooth the language, remove redundancies, and reconcile differences of interpretation. We've also reduced the page total of the original cases by roughly a third. The result, we hope, is a text that continues to highlight the managerial issues and lessons of the telecommunications reorganizations but that is also readable.

A word about authorship. The entire series was created under the direction of Leonard A. Schlesinger, who has presided over its own reorganization and adaptation from the beginning. Schlesinger and James L. Wilson wrote the first draft of the case here appearing as chapters 1 and 2. Davis Dyer adapted that material and wrote the case that appears here in modified form as chapter 6. Thomas N. Clough was responsible for the cases on which chapters 4, 5, and 7 are based. Dyer and Clough together wrote the material that forms the basis of chapters 3 and 10. Diane Landau wrote chapters 8 and 9 and the appendix, and, under the direction of Schlesinger and Dyer, edited the entire book and drafted the framing material for each section. Clough and Dyer wrote the afterword based on material prepared by Landau and discussions of the entire group.

The authors are grateful for the support and encouragement of the Division of Research at the Harvard Business School, particularly from Professor E. Raymond Corey, director from 1980 to 1985, and Dean John H. McArthur. Many employees and former employees of AT&T—W. Brooke Tunstall, Robert Lloyd, Curtis Garner—supplied information and insights and helped arrange interviews. Robert G. Lewis, Robert W. Garnet, and Alan Gardner of AT&T commented critically and helpfully on an early draft of this manuscript. At Northwestern Bell and U S WEST, Jack MacAllister has been a firm supporter of the project. John Felt of U S WEST also provided valuable assistance. Finally, we would also like to thank many colleagues who helped shape the case series as contributors, advisers, and teachers, including especially Paul Lawrence, Anthony Oettinger, Richard Vietor, and James L. Wilson.

Directory of Names

Robert E. Allen — Chairman of AT&T Informational Systems

Gary Ames — Vice-president and treasurer, U S WEST

Robert Beck — Assistant vice-president for human resources, staffing, and development at AT&T

Charles L. Brown — Chairman of AT&T, 1978–1986

Don Buxton* — Manager, residence segment, in Minnesota and head of Northwestern Bell task force on management structure

Robert Casale — Assistant vice-president and national director, business sales, at AT&T

John deButts — Chairman of AT&T, 1972–1978

Howard Doerr — Executive vice-president and chief financial officer of U S WEST. Earlier CFO at Northwestern Bell

William Ellinghaus — President of AT&T

John Felt — Vice-president–public relations, at U S WEST

Individuals' titles refer to positions held at time of last mention in the text. An asterisk indicates a disguised name.

John Howard*   Vice-president–business segment, at
                                Northwestern Bell

Larry Kappel   Vice-president–strategic planning, at
                                U S WEST in 1984. Earlier strategic
                                planner at Northwestern Bell

Jack MacAllister   President and CEO of U S WEST.
                                Earlier president of Northwestern
                                Bell

Dick McCormick   President of Northwestern Bell.
                                Earlier vice-president of network
                                operations

Arch McGill   Vice-president–business marketing at
                                AT&T

Charles Marshall   Corporate executive vice-president
                                for personnel and external affairs

Ted Meridith*   State CEO of Minnesota for
                                Northwestern Bell

James Olson   Vice-chairman of AT&T

Alfred C. Partoll   Vice-president–state regulatory
                                affairs at AT&T

Bill Roberts*   Senior vice-president–business at
                                Northwestern Bell

H. I. Romnes   Chairman of AT&T, 1967–1972

Jean Smith*   Vice-president–personnel at
                                Northwestern Bell

Brooke W. Tunstall   Vice-president–corporate planning at
                                AT&T

Alvin von Auw   Vice-president and assistant to the
                                chairman of AT&T

Theodore N. Vail   President of AT&T (1907–1919) and
                                earlier general manager of American
                                Bell who articulated strategy of
                                universal service and systems
                                communications

Chronicles
of
Corporate
Change

———

Part I
Stability

In the late 1870s, Theodore Vail, general manager of the American Bell Telephone Company, formulated the strategy and designed the structure that underlay the rise of the Bell System from a Boston household firm to its position a century later as the world's largest and wealthiest private corporation. For most of that century Vail's ideas served the company well. The Bell System strategy was to provide universal low-cost telephone service, and its structure was vertically integrated organization by function.

The changes that forced AT&T to reevaluate its traditional strategy and structure came in the 1960s. New technologies, the unabated growth of the telecommunications industry, the advent of competition, and a new willingness of regulatory agencies to foster competition all combined dramatically to alter the business environment. To understand AT&T and the magnitude of the problems presented by a major reorganization, it is helpful to review the forces that shaped the company's traditional strategy and structure.

The Bell System's functional organization was laid out in its first decade of operation. By the mid-1880s, the System's structure as a holding company with centralized manufacturing, research and design, coordination of long-distance service, and decentralized operating companies was roughly in place. As president after 1907, Vail set up the more particular functional organization of AT&T's general departments and of the Bell Operating Companies (BOCs). The company had slowly been gathering the geographically scattered BOCs into a single system with standardized engineering and operating procedures. After 1909, both AT&T and the BOCs adopted similar departmental structures based on functional skills.

Table I–1
The Bell System, 1913–1973

Industry environment:	Stable. Regulated monopoly status. No significant competition. Controlled pace of technological change.
Policy environment:	Stable with overlapping jurisdictions between the FCC (after 1934), state public utility commissions, and federal courts.
Regulatory justification:	Natural monopoly (technological standardization and efficiency).
Regulatory challenges:	Rate of return regulation. Antitrust investigations.
Pressures for change:	Limited before late 1960s. Then service crises, unfavorable regulatory rulings raise concerns.
Key management problem:	Growth and integration of national telephone network.
Internal environment and capacity for change:	Stable corporate environment. Growing organization. Little need to change.

Operators served in one department (traffic), tool-handling craftsmen in another (plant), technical experts in a third (engineering), and customer relations people in the fourth (commercial). This structure was successful in the benign regulatory environment and produced a stability in the Bell System's organization that lasted over sixty years.

By the 1960s, however, population growth had increased telephone usage and greater internal coordination was needed throughout the System. New telecommunications technologies developed rapidly inside and outside the Bell System, while new entrants threatened to erode Bell's natural monopoly. Public regulatory agencies began to question the industry and particularly, its leading player.

By the early 1970s AT&T's functional structure proved inadequate to the new demands. Embarrassing service crises and small but growing losses of orders to business customers caused senior executives to reexamine assumptions in the management structure, and in late 1972 AT&T's highest officers, the Executive Policy Committee, requested the headquarters planning staff to prepare a comprehensive study of the Bell System's structure, suggesting changes where appropriate, to bring the System's organization in line with its new environment. The corporate planners prescribed three alternatives: AT&T could retain its traditional organization; it could move directly to a competitive, market-oriented structure; or it could adopt a hybrid, transitional form combining features of the other two alternatives.

Chapter 1 describes the development of AT&T's traditional strategy and structure to the early 1970s. Chapter 2 discusses the forces transforming the telecommunications industry and outlines AT&T's initial response to these changes. Table I–1, summarizing AT&T's business and regulatory environment and its management challenges during its first century, may be used as a reference guide to chapters 1 and 2.

1

A Century of Corporate Development

The first century of Bell System history breaks down into three periods. From 1875 to 1894, the company flourished as a monopoly protected by the patent laws. In the second period (1894–1913), the Bell System struggled in competition with other telephone companies, although it relied increasingly on the development of its long-distance network and its managerial experience to retain its competitive advantage. The organizational pattern of the holding company and the structural relations between the parent and the associated companies were formalized during this competitive period. In the third period (1913 to the mid-1970s), AT&T resided fairly comfortably in an organizational and strategic equilibrium with its environment under state and federal regulation.

Alexander Graham Bell discovered the means to send and receive voice transmissions over wire in 1875, and during their first nineteen years the Bell companies used the U.S. patent laws to shield Bell from competition. Gardiner G. Hubbard, an attorney and Bell's father-in-law, managed the developing company's first business in Boston. According to company tradition, it was Hubbard who helped make the decision to exploit the patent by renting rather than selling telephone equipment.[1] Despite this wise business decision, chronic shortages of capital inhibited Bell's abilities to develop and market the telephone, so Bell's early managers responded with an innovative organizational structure. To set up a business beyond the confines of Boston, Bell managers arranged for agents to provide service and collect revenues under temporary licensing agreements. (This was the germ of the future relationship between AT&T and the BOCs). To attract capital, the associates shared control of the business early with outside investors and managers, primarily bankers.

One of the first outside managers brought in was Theodore Vail, a young man with considerable experience in the telegraph business and railway mail service. Vail's early career had taught him both the importance of systems and networks and the value of thinking big. Within a few weeks of his arrival at American Bell, he understood that "it is more the system established in connection with the telephone, than the telephone itself, that makes the value of the telephone."[2] Accordingly, in 1881 the company scrapped the loose coalition of temporary agencies and eventually granted permanent licenses to build and operate telephone exchanges in return for a 30 to 50 percent equity interest in the licensee.[3] He later urged the parent company to acquire a higher percentage of stock whenever possible.

Bell executives took advantage of patent protection to prepare the company for later dominance in the business. Looking ahead to the expiration of the original patents, Vail persuaded American Bell to buy up new patents for the emerging switchboard and exchange technologies. Vail and his associate E. J. Hall also encouraged the company to develop a long-distance business. The first long-distance call was placed between Boston and Lowell in 1879. "What we wanted to do," Vail said later, "was to get possession of the field in such a way that, patent or no patent, we could control it."[4] Vail also saw the need to secure a steady supply of equipment for the emerging business. Thus, in 1882 he arranged the purchase of an important electrical equipment manufacturer in the Midwest, the Western Electric Company, which had previously supplied apparatus to Western Union, the telegraph monopoly.

By the early 1880s, then, American Bell was vertically integrated with a centralized headquarters staff and management of long-distance business, manufacturing, and research and development (R&D). The company's need to adapt to competition and growth after 1894 prompted subsequent organizational changes. Independent companies immediately began to form in areas not yet served by Bell. Eighty-seven companies entered the telephone business in 1894. Clever entrepreneurs took advantage of popular indignation with the telephone company's high rental charges. By 1902 a federal census showed more than fifteen hundred independent companies controlling 1.5 million miles of wire and 1.05 million telephones. In the same year the Bell companies operated 3.4 million miles of wire and 1.3 million telephones. Competition was fierce and sometimes unethical; questionable tactics included predatory pricing and secret takeovers. Other tactics, however, included acquisitions, expansion, propaganda, litigation, refusal to sell equipment, and refusal to interconnect with the independents.

Several factors worked in American Bell's favor to change this competitive position. First, only American Bell offered long-distance service. It was easy enough for independent companies to start up, quite another matter for them to grow beyond their local borders. Indeed, the technology, capital, and managerial experience needed to integrate the long-distance business and the local exchange led to a structural reorganization of the Bell System itself in the 1890s.

Since 1885, a subsidiary of American Bell known as the American Telephone and Telegraph Company had managed long-distance traffic. In 1899 AT&T became the parent company in a two-for-one stock swap with American Bell and moved from Boston to New York. The shift permitted AT&T to take advantage of proximity to the capital markets as well as New York's more liberal corporation laws, but it also brought the Bell System's organization more into line with its actual workings. AT&T had produced nearly half of system revenues and had provided the central point of contact between headquarters and the BOCs. When J. P. Morgan took over AT&T in 1907, his interests supported Theodore Vail's perspectives. With an antipathy to competition, Morgan's new strategy called for the system to grow by acquisition rather than by cutthroat competition and duplication of service.

AT&T's image at the turn of the century was that of a "ruthless, grinding, oppressive monopoly."[5] As a result, the first public agencies, which had formed in Wisconsin and New York in 1907 to set railroad rates, started monitoring telephone rates. The federal government began to look askance at AT&T's size, too, especially after Vail arranged a merger with Western Union in 1909. The Interstate

Commerce Commission (ICC) undertook federal auditing of telephone accounts in 1910. As soon as it took office, the Wilson administration launched an antitrust investigation against AT&T. With the inconvenience and wastefulness of competing exchanges that did not interconnect, public pressure mounted. Communications, they cried, was a natural monopoly, and open competition was a duplicative industry structure for the patented tool.

The public pressure led to a historic concession. N. C. Kingsbury, an AT&T vice-president, signed an agreement with the government to dispose of the company's controlling interest in Western Union, to forswear future acquisitions of the independents without ICC approval, and to interconnect with all responsible independent companies.

As president from 1907 to 1919, Vail added several important innovations to the Bell System's organization.[6] First, Vail and E. J. Hall set off AT&T's operating company segment from its holding company for BOC stock. Next, Vail, together with John J. Carty, standardized system research and development. Prior to 1907 each of the BOCs and Western Electric had maintained its own research staff and had dabbled in new products; Vail and Carty centralized R&D at headquarters and defined clear procedures and standards for all parts of the system. AT&T issued corporate guidelines that kept each of the BOCs in line with the general departments at headquarters, and switched their operations from a geographical to a functional perspective. Now, each BOC was instructed to set up plant, traffic, and commercial departments within each local district and to report on a dotted-line basis to the corresponding departments at AT&T. Soon afterwards, most of the companies in the system added engineering departments with the same reporting arrangement.

Much as Vail shaped the organization of AT&T, he also defined its strategy. As early as 1879 he had emphasized the need to build the telephone business into a national system. In one of his first annual presidential reports in 1908, he pronounced the company's goal to be "one system, one policy, universal service." This emphasis on service was later crystallized by one of Vail's successors, W. S. Gifford, who proclaimed in 1927 that the mission of the Bell System was "to furnish the best possible service at the lowest possible cost consistent with financial safety."[7]

Yet, the manner in which AT&T set about reaching this goal changed over time. In the beginning, the company adopted a manufacturing strategy to produce standardized products and depended on economies of scale to keep costs low. Later, as a result of a new public policy in the early 1940s, the System applied revenues from long-distance services to support local exchanges (cross-subsidies).

Equilibrium

For nearly six decades the Bell System reposed in an adaptive equilibrium with its external environment despite two massive antitrust suits, the intense and hostile scrutiny of the FCC, and frequent attacks by muckraking journalists and authors. The most serious problems stemmed from two antitrust suits filed in 1913 and 1949 and an exceedingly thorough FCC investigation in the 1930s. AT&T emerged from each of these ruffled but intact. The government did nationalize telephone and telegraph service for a brief period (1918–1919) but eventually conceded that private management was more efficient. The FCC investigation, the first after its founding in 1934, led to no substantive public policy changes but did reinforce the public's image of AT&T as a giant company sprawling out of control. The second antitrust case (1949–1956), aimed at breaking up AT&T's vertical integration by forcing divestiture of Western Electric, instead generated an opposite result. AT&T was permitted to retain its manufacturing division, Western Electric, but the BOCs were limited to the business of providing voice communications services.

The settlement proved costly as communications and data-processing services began to overlap, but it did legitimize AT&T's basic organization as a holding company. The passage of time brought little challenge to AT&T's fundamental strategy or structure, since the company was shielded from competition by the natural-monopoly regulation. The significant organizational innovations of these sixty years were the formal establishment of Bell Labs in 1925 out of Western Electric's engineering department, and the creation of a small marketing unit at headquarters in 1959.

Internally, the organization adjusted and responded to environmental change. During World War II, the company contributed heavily to national defense while forgoing all but essential maintenance of the telephone network. The status of the rate-setting departments grew during a financial crisis that followed the war. The FCC froze rates and squeezed the corporation's costs and profits; by 1946, AT&T's stock was depressed and its only means to attract new capital was long-term borrowing. In the next two years the debt-to-equity ratio rose from a traditional 33 percent to 50 percent, and the company faced serious financial trouble. The hard-driving leadership of President Leroy A. Wilson and vigorous pressure on various public agencies eventually won rate hikes, allowing AT&T to increase its return on capital and its stock price. Nevertheless, this brush with financial disaster left an indelible mark on AT&T's management.

The years of organizational and strategic stasis tended to breed a conservative and unchanging management style within the corporation. From the very beginning, most of AT&T's senior managers sprang from blueblood backgrounds; they were Boston Brahmins and Ivy Leaguers. Over the years more and more engineers became high officers, but AT&T executives still prided themselves on their humanist heritage. Vice-presidents were as likely to quote from Shakespeare and the classics as from Peter Drucker. A formal training program of the 1950s even sent managers back to school at the University of Pennsylvania, Swarthmore, and Darthmouth for liberal arts courses. However, as was true of most older industrial organizations in the United States, management training was more often in house and on the job. Senior managers generally spent their entire careers in the Bell System, and almost all of the very highest circulated through one of the BOCs, Western Electric, or Bell Labs before returning to headquarters.

The traditional organizational style of AT&T up to the mid-1970s was well captured by writer John Brooks:

> There is a certain sameness about AT&T people. Their dress and manner is conservative, but not to the point of stuffiness. . . . They seem far more vivid, dashing, and enterprising than a building full of government bureaucrats, but far less so than, say, the brainy and hungry young hotshots of some rising new high-technology company. . . . Top AT&T people's tastes and interests tend to be similar, and for those who are going places, their primary interest is the Bell System. . . . Life at 195 [Broadway—company head-

quarters in New York], on the surface at least, is bland and civil; only very occasionally does one catch a whiff of the corporate jungle. . . .[8]

Nowhere was this genteel business spirit better illustrated than in the Bell System's approach to sales and marketing. The company expected its sales force to respond to customer needs rather than to anticipate them. It also expected sales representatives to fit the customer to existing communications services rather than adapt or create a product for a particular market. Sales reps were charged to provide advice to customers who typically had little technical knowledge of communications and to arrange for a mix of standard products and services that met the customers' needs; any business a sales rep drummed up was called an "artificial" sale. Bell's sales reps were paid a straight salary and were unlikely to rise high in the company hierarchy. One senior AT&T spokesman remembered that these sales policies stemmed from a desire to "avoid incentives that might tempt sales personnel to overload customers with unnecessary equipment."[9] AT&T's principal marketing tools were periodic product bulletins that flowed from company headquarters. Until 1974 there was no systematic mechanism for evaluating customer desires.

Since Vail's time, AT&T's annual reports have spelled out its corporate philosophy of service to the public and commitment to high-quality, reliable technology (see figure 1-1 for one such statement by Chairman H. I. Romnes in 1971). In the words of one senior executive, "The Bell System's basic aim has been and continues to be the widest availability of high-quality communications services at the lowest overall cost to the entire public. It is the aim that governs the design of our services and the way they are marketed and priced." AT&T considers the telephone network and Bell Labs to be "a unique national resource," and it speaks proudly of its responsibility for managing "the best telephone service in the world."

Regulation

During the six decades after 1913, state public utility commissions (PUCs) and the FCC (after 1934) regulated a relatively stable and

Our first responsibility today remains what it has always been: service to the public. It is the Bell System's objective to provide the best possible communications service we know how to give and to do so at the most reasonable rates over the long run. . . . The United States is almost alone among the nations of the world in entrusting the development and the operation of its communications services to private enterprise. Thus the realistic need to insure profitability through improved efficiency and continuous innovation is as strong a motivation in our business as it is in any other. And it is largely to this motivation that our nation owes the present scope and versatility of its comunications services and their low cost. In short, it is our commitment to service that requires that we earn profits that will justify the continuing confidence of investors in our business. It is the commitment that requires that our financing policies take first account of the interest of our existing share owners and the need to maintain the integrity of their investment. It requires that we set as our goal earnings that are comparable with those of other industries of like risk and like prospects. It requires that we pay dividends that are generally within the range paid out by other progressive, growing businesses. It requires that we continuously increase the earning power of our shares, by profitably reinvesting in the business that portion of our earnings that remains after dividends. At the same time, it requires that we shun any action that is merely expedient, offering temporary advantage or momentary favor at the cost of sound long-term growth. But when all is said and done, our responsibility to investors places no greater obligation on us than this: that we address ourselves continuously to the enhancement of our business's capabilities and the value of our service to the public.

We have some other responsibilities too. They are not new, but some of them are newly urgent in the public mind. We have a responsibility to be good citizens in the communities we serve. It is basic to this responsibility that we extend every reasonable effort to be sure that our facilities enhance and do not impair the physical environment in which we operate. But beyond that we have a responsibility to the future—to do what we can to help restore where it has been lost—and maintain where it has not—a social environment in which we can do our best.

> Finally, we have responsibilities to the nation at large: first, to take scrupulous account of the consequences of what we do on the general economy; second, to respond to the nation's needs whenever and wherever our skills are truly needed; and third, to give our wholehearted support to the great goals our country has set for itself: a growing economy, a decent order in our society, the freedom and scope for every individual to fulfill his personal capacities, and an environment that will sustain the continuing enhancement of the quality of our national life.
>
> —H. I. Romnes
> *From remarks at the Annual Meeting of Share Owners,*
> *Dallas, Texas, April 22, 1971*

Source: AT&T Annual Report, 1971.

Figure 1–1. *Statement of AT&T Philosophy, 1971*

predictable business, which provided a single service: voice communications. The regulators and the public considered the industry to be a natural monopoly, and AT&T managed itself following usual regulatory guidelines. In Vail's words, the character of the regulation should be

> such . . . as to encourage the highest possible standard in plant, the utmost extension of facilities, the highest efficiency in service, and to that end should allow rates that will warrant the highest wages for the best service, some reward for high efficiency in administration, and such certainty of return on investment as will induce investors . . . to supply all the capital needed to meet the demands of the public.[10]

State and federal policy allowed AT&T to retrieve its capital and labor expenses and still achieve "a fair rate of return" on investment in network expansion—usually 5 to 7 percent. The PUCs set tariffs (rental fees) for telephone equipment and rates for local service and intrastate telephone calls, and the FCC set rates on interstate calls and acted as the voice of federal public policy toward the industry. Thus, AT&T's relationship with both the PUCs and the FCC was highly sensitive.

In its early years, the FCC gave more concern to issues of broadcast communications than to telephones. Indeed, the commission's Common Carrier Bureau, responsible for telephone regulation, is one of five bureaus of equal administrative standing. In 1974 it employed only 227 persons, about one-tenth of total staff at the FCC.[11] In the late 1970s, the FCC acted to open up industry competition. The changed outlook in response to the emergence of new technologies, the availability of new customer products, and consumers' new demands forced AT&T to undertake a critical appraisal of organizational structure and corporate strategies.

Bell System Organization

By the early 1970s, AT&T ranked as one of the largest private organizations in the world, employing more than a million people and with total assets of more than $75 billion. AT&T was a vertically integrated holding company, controlling the telephone business at every stage from the purchase of raw materials to the distribution of service. AT&T oversaw twenty-three operating companies, one of the largest private research laboratories in the world, its own massive manufacturing organization, and a long-distance communications network that linked customers throughout the country to each other and to communications networks overseas. The entire system was coordinated from corporate headquarters in New York City and in Basking Ridge, New Jersey (see figure 1–2). And Theodore Vail's 1917 system endured; AT&T still was

> primarily a holding company, holding stocks of the associated operating and manufacturing companies. As an operating company it owns and operates the long-distance lines, the lines that connect all the systems of the associated operating companies with each other. In addition . . . it assumes what might be termed the centralized general administrative functions of all the associated companies. . . .[12]

AT&T's general operations staff is shown in figure 1–3; heading up the organization are the chairman and the board of directors.

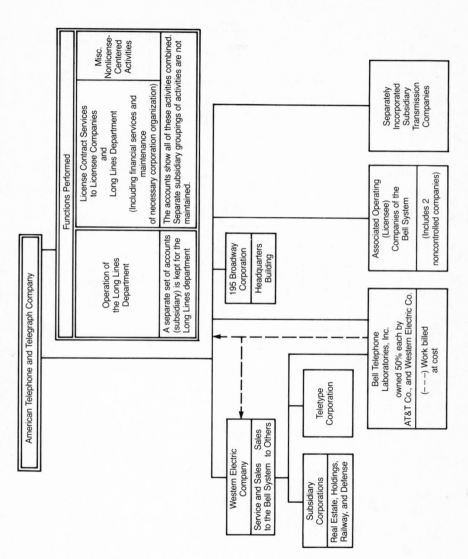

Figure 1–2. *Functional Organization of the Bell System in the 1970s*

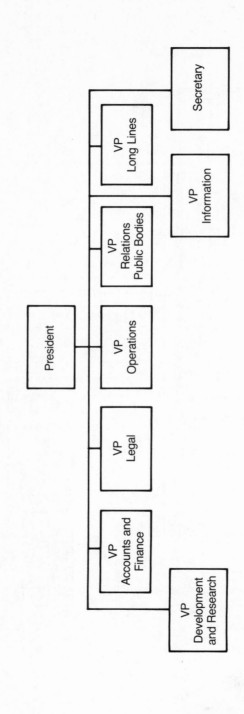

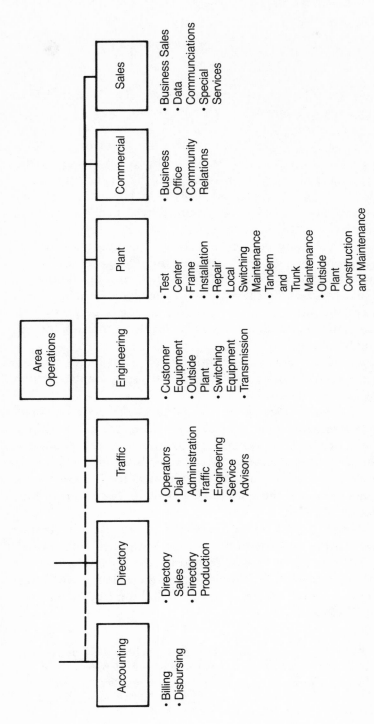

Figure 1–3. *Traditional Structure of AT&T and BOCs*

The president served as chief executive officer (CEO) until 1961, when the chairman became CEO; chief operating duties were then assigned to the president and later to a vice-chairman.

In the first decade after the bankers acquired control of AT&T in 1907, the board exerted considerable influence on management, especially in financial matters. In the 1920s the board's influence diminished. Since then, the role of professional management has increased steadily, and by 1970 corporate staff at headquarters included more than ten thousand managers.

For most of the twentieth century, AT&T business was divided between telephone services and transmission. The general departments provided services to the BOCs: research and development, advice and assistance to their functional departments, and legal and financial help including assistance in marketing securities. The Long Lines department managed domestic and international long-distance telephone traffic.

Over the years there was some shifting of responsibility, and by 1974 the general departments and Long Lines were combined under the purview of a vice-chairman.

Despite its regulated status, in 1959 AT&T developed a small marketing department, which was closely tied to traditional functions. The engineering department remained responsible for long-range planning, with the entire network's needs foremost in mind. In 1970 a new emphasis on customer service resulted in a corporate staff reorganization, and the sales force was removed from the marketing department to the general departments.

The Western Electric Company, which had been AT&T's major supplier since 1882, was the largest single component of the Bell System. Were it a free-standing company, Western would have ranked as the nation's twelfth-largest industrial in 1972, with over 200,000 employees and sales in excess of $7 billion. Its general role, as the 1939 FCC study put it,

> is two-fold: First, it is the manufacturing branch of the Bell System; and second, it is the purchasing and supply department of the Bell System. In connection with its latter function, Western Electric is also a developer, storekeeper, installer, repairer, salvager, and junker of the Bell System. . . .[13]

After the 1956 consent decree, which restricted AT&T from entering data-processing businesses, Western sold primarily within the Bell System. Because it had such a large assured market, Western's manufacturing strategy was to standardize product lines, count on extended production runs, and capitalize on enormous economies of scale. Western's relationship to the System was one way, however, since AT&T, Bell Labs, and the BOCs were not obliged to purchase from it. Indeed, the percentage of equipment the System purchased from Western had fallen steadily, from more than 90 percent in the early 1960s to less than 85 percent by the mid-1970s.

The Bell Telephone Laboratories were formed out of the Western Electric engineering research department in 1925 and were jointly owned by Western and AT&T, with a fifty-fifty split. Bell Labs had produced on average more than one patent every working day since its founding. The list of significant discoveries and innovations produced by Bell Labs—radio equipment, radar, waveguide transmission, transistors, semiconductors, fiber optics, lasers, and electronic switching equipment—supported a reputation as the world's best and most prolific research and development institution. In the early 1970s the Labs operated in seventeen locations, employed some 17,000 people, including 2,000 with Ph.D.'s., and managed an annual budget in excess of $500 million. Like the rest of the Bell System, the Labs preferred to develop their own personnel; they normally hired scientists and engineers fresh out of school.

Because the Bell System's regulated environment shielded it from competition for many years, the company felt little pressure to develop innovations quickly. By tradition, Bell Labs initiated their own projects, although they needed approval by AT&T. Instead of targeting innovation to the System's operational needs, the Labs often focused on basic research, affecting System architecture very slowly, first generating new technical concepts and only then looking for applications. As an AT&T marketing executive said in 1970, "Prior to competition we introduced things when we were good and ready."[14]

While the Labs clearly were leaders in communications technology, their efforts were remote from System operations and customers. An extreme example of the Labs' lack of market sensitivity was the Picturephone, an effort to combine closed-circuit television and the telephone. The multimillion-dollar product was readied and introduced in 1969, with projected sales in the billions of dollars. To AT&T's chagrin, however, virtually no demand for the product was found, then or in later years. At AT&T vice-president for engineering and a former Bell Labs employee commented in 1974 on this isolation from the marketplace: "I could hope," he said, "that in the future, Bell Labs would get out more and find out what the real telephone world is like."[15]

In 1973 AT&T owned 100 percent of the stock of 17 of the 23 regional operating companies, controlling interest in 4 others, and minority shares in 2 cases (see figure 1–4). Each company, regardless of its ownership, paid AT&T 2 percent of its gross revenues under a license contract, which obligated AT&T to maintain the long-distance network, manage a central staff, and conduct research and development.

But the parent company's supervision over the BOCs developed into a tightly bound relationship:

> In exercising its control over these regional subsidiaries, [AT&T] licenses their operation under its patents, controls their financing; elects their directors; appoints their officers; directs their rate-making advertising and public relations policies; standardizes their equipment; requires them to render periodic reports; and checks the latter by means of traveling auditors.[16]

Each BOC's organization was based on functional skills and mirrored that of AT&T's general departments. The commercial department's work included rate negotiations with the PUCs, revenue collection, advertising, publication of directories, and routine customer relations. The plant department built and maintained central offices and performed routine wiring and installation. The engineering department enforced Bell System engineering standards and handled technical problems requiring special skills. The traffic department included operator services and personnel responsible for smoothing the flow of telephone traffic. In addition, each BOC had a separate accounting function. Individual careers normally developed exclusively within these departments, and functional differentiation extended up through several levels of management before

Name	Area Served
New England Telephone & Telegraph Company	Maine, Massachusetts, New Hampshire, Rhode Island, Vermont
The Southern New England Telephone Company	Connecticut
New York Telephone Company	New York, portion of Connecticut
New Jersey Bell Telephone Company	New Jersey
The Bell Telephone Company of Pennsylvania	Pennsylvania
The Diamond State Telephone Company	Delaware
The Chesapeake and Potomac Telephone Company	Washington, D.C.
The Chesapeake and Potomac Telephone Company of Maryland	Maryland
The Chesapeake and Potomac Telephone Company of Virginia	Virginia
The Chesapeake and Potomac Telephone Company of West Virginia	West Virginia
Southern Bell Telephone and Telegraph Company	Florida, Georgia, North Carolina, South Carolina
South Central Bell Telephone Company	Alabama, Kentucky, Louisiana, Mississippi, Tennessee
The Ohio Bell Telephone Company	Ohio
Cincinnati Bell Inc.	Cincinnati, portions of Kentucky, Indiana
Michigan Bell Telephone Company	Michigan
Indiana Bell Telephone Company, Incorporated	Indiana
Wisconsin Telephone Company	Wisconsin
Illinois Bell Telephone Company	Illinois, portion of Indiana
Northwestern Bell Telephone Company	Iowa, Minnesota, Nebraska, North Dakota, South Dakota
Southwestern Bell Telephone Company	Arkansas, Kansas, Missouri, Oklahoma, Texas
The Mountain States Telephone and Telegraph Company	Arizona, Colorado, Idaho, Montana, New Mexico, Utah, Wyoming, portion of Texas
Pacific Northwest Bell Telephone Company	Oregon, Washington, portion of Idaho
The Pacific Telephone and Telegraph Company (including Bell Telephone Company of Nevada)	California, Nevada

Source: AT&T Annual Report, 1978.

Figure 1–4. *Bell System Subsidiaries, 1978*

general coordination began at the level of vice-president—operations. Nevertheless, over the years AT&T's tight supervision of the BOCs eroded. Despite the need for a close working relationship, recent AT&T executives prided themselves that they seldom issued direct orders to the BOC presidents, who in turn prided themselves on their independence. Said one BOC president:

> We are pretty much left to our own devices. . . . On the other hand, I have heard from some of my colleagues—other Bell operating company presidents—that when there is serious trouble they are apt to get a kind of supervision that I, personally, wouldn't care for. . . . In the end, a lot flows back to earnings: if your earnings are good, AT&T is very permissive; if not, it isn't.[17]

Changing relationships between AT&T and the BOCs eventually weakened the System's organizational bonds. By the early 1970s, the tight coordination and parallel structures of headquarters and subsidiaries had almost disappeared. In 1973 only seven BOCs retained the traditional functional structure in its original form.

Costs and Controls

Although AT&T earned about $17 million per day after taxes in 1980, these profits did not result from the control of costs and prices. Regulation had afforded the company an ability to develop complex and interdependent accounting practices. AT&T never linked its services with specific costs and revenues; rather, the company treated all revenues as one homogeneous stream, and responsibility for profits in the functional structure fell to the highest executives. Lower managers were evaluated and rewarded on their ability to reduce costs per standard task while continuing to meet service quality standards. There were no uniform methods for allocating joint costs despite the legal fact that more than 90 percent of AT&T's total investment in plant was shared across state and federal jurisdictions.

In principle, the policy of cost allocation and revenue settlements (also known as separations and settlements) attempted to resolve this problem. Every telephone call that extended beyond the local exchange potentially affected three different parts of the Bell System. A long-distance call between New York and Chicago, for example, involved the originating exchange (New York Telephone), AT&T Long Lines, and the terminating exchange (Illinois Bell). The accountants' problem at AT&T was how to separate these costs and allocate revenues when it was impossible to distinguish among them. Telephones and local wires were "usage insensitive"; that is, the costs of maintaining them were indifferent to the amount and kind of use they received. Thus, separating costs between the local exchange and the long-distance exchange became highly arbitrary.

In addition to the allocation confusion, cross-subsidies between services complicated accounting procedures. First, for political reasons, the state PUCs tried to keep rates for residential users as low as possible, while favoring rate hikes for business customers. This policy, in effect, encouraged AT&T to subsidize residential rates at the expense of commercial users. Second, the FCC had ordered nationwide rate averaging for long-distance service. Thus the revenues from low-density routes, which may only partially cover their operating costs, were pooled with the revenues of high-density routes, which may exceed operating costs. Costs were then averaged and shared. Finally, federal and state regulatory policies encouraged cross-subsidies between local and long-distance exchanges. In practice, rates for local service were kept uniform and low at the expense of long-distance customers. As an AT&T vice-president explained: "The average revenue for an interstate message is $2.25. About 75 cents of that is used to support local exchange charges beyond the cost of transmission."

That 75 cents represented a 25 percent subsidy to the local exchange, a percentage arbitrarily fixed by regulators and often varying from jurisdiction to jurisdiction. The separations and settlements policy, though meritorious from a public policy perspective because it permitted almost everyone to afford a telephone and allowed the establishment of a national network, was more dubious in pure economic terms. Any method AT&T and its regulators chose was arbitrary. It was impossible to isolate the "true" costs of providing telephone service.

AT&T continued to support the separations policy for two reasons: it allowed the company to standardize accounting procedures and rates across all the BOCs, while also helping to target techno-logical innovation on long-distance service. The new transmission techniques, increased capacity of cables, and more elegant ways of switching had reduced the costs of long-distance service dramati-cally while rates had declined somewhat less. The company made its money on long-distance traffic and could afford to subsidize its less-profitable operations without a drop in earnings.

AT&T was also subject to public policy in its accounting for depreciation. Regulatory agencies required AT&T to depreciate its assets on a straight-line basis over as long a period as possible. Therefore, most assets were depreciated over their useful lives (up to eighty years) rather than their economic lives. Such timetables encouraged AT&T to increase investment in plant steadily as the network expanded, but those same timetables also discouraged in-novation. Installation of new technology became economically fea-sible only when expansion was required or when equipment in place was used for a substantial fraction of its accounting life. Although technological advances could offer a means of providing service at a lower cost, product introductions were sometimes delayed as at-tendance to regulatory accounting rules took precedence over cost control and competitive pricing.

Because of long depreciation schedules, early replacement of plant caused huge write-offs, which tended to lower profits or raise rates. Lower profits could make AT&T a less desirable investment and complicated the job of raising almost $4 billion in capital per year; higher rates could put AT&T at a competitive disadvantage. In the 1970s, when the economic lives of electronic equipment were sometimes measured in months, AT&T's imposed depreciation pol-icies became increasingly inappropriate.

By the 1970s, the strategy, structure, and management systems that had served AT&T so well during most of the twentieth century were proving inadequate to match the complexity of its business environment. New technologies, combined with the massive growth of the industry and a new willingness of public policy makers to change the rules of regulation, led top management to reassess the direction of the Bell System in the coming decade.

2
Portents of Change

From its inception, the Bell System maintained a conservative management style, which supported its ability to provide universal, low-cost telephone service to nationwide users. As a government-regulated utility, Bell achieved its objectives through an organization that was vertically integrated by function. As the original corporate goal of universal service was achieved, however, and as new technologies led to changes in the regulatory and competitive environment, AT&T was forced to reconsider its traditional strategy and structure. By 1970, 92 percent of domestic households included at least one telephone, leaving little opportunity for growth in residential markets beyond improvements in service. Thus top management confronted a problem with two dimensions: AT&T had to get the Bell System moving to capture new business markets while also upholding its corporate image to the public as a high-quality service organization. Less visibly, the company began to prepare itself to survive in a competitive world.

The Changing Telecommunications Industry

By the mid-1970s, telecommunications was one of the largest and most concentrated industries in the country. Total revenues had reached some $35 billion and were growing at more than 11 percent per year; the Bell System's total market share held constant at about 80 percent. However, AT&T's secure position was beginning to erode. Forces of change included new technologies of transmission, increasing sophistication of customer premises equipment, dramatic growth in the volume of business, and availability of competitive services and products outside the Bell System. At the same time, regulatory agencies showed a new willingness not only to tolerate but actually to promote competition.

Telecommunications technology is divided into three horizontal functions: customer premises equipment, the local exchange, and long-distance services.[18] *Customer premises equipment* includes telephones and teletypes. Increasingly, in business applications it also includes private branch exchanges (PBXs—electronic switchboards with advanced customer features), the so-called smart phone, and programmable terminals (computers). The *local exchange* includes local central switching offices and cables from them to the customer premises. *Long-distance services* refers to the technology linking local loops into intrastate, interstate, and international networks.

For most of AT&T's history, a tight fit existed among these horizontal functions, Bell System strategy, and the company's vertical organization. Western Electric and the BOCs supplied and managed customer premises equipment and the local exchange, while AT&T Long Lines managed long-distance service. The company's natural monopoly extended to all three horizontal functions.

In the 1970s, however, new technologies were straining Bell System organization at every point. In customer premises equipment, the distinction between the previously separate functions of data *transmission* and data *processing*—in lay terms, between telephones and computers—was blurring. The traditional method of voice transmission used analog signals, whereby the actual voice modulation was directly converted into electrical impulses along a continuous wave of varying strength and duration by the transmitter, and later reconverted by the receiver. Technological developments of the 1970s allowed voice inputs to be converted into digital values and packed together for transmission. Thus, what was essentially a digital computer sat at either end of a telephone call, and transmission methods became computerized. A so-called smart telephone could now use the digital technologies for both information transmission *and* information processing.

In the local exchange, product migration—PBXs and advanced switching systems—removed switching from the central office to customer premises and began eroding businesses' boundary between customer premises equipment and the local exchange. Additionally, the local network's natural monopoly was challenged as citizens band (CB) radio and pocket page services were able to bypass the local loop, thus invalidating natural monopoly justifications. One of AT&T's own products in development, the Advanced Mobile Communication Service, portended a future telephone without wires. Domestic satellites with rooftop or neighborhood receiving stations presented alternatives to the entrenched network, complemented by the development of cable television with possible videotext services.

AT&T's monopoly on long-distance exchange was also challenged. A handful of satellites could literally replace the entire longlines capacity of the terrestrial network, and the corporation was aware of the competitive implications posed by other carriers' longdistance microwave radio transmission. Indeed, competitors had already tapped both business and residential markets with the service. In this process, high-frequency signals were transmitted between radio dishes mounted on tall buildings or towers at intervals of about thirty miles. The Bell System itself had a heavy investment in microwave, which accounted for nearly half of the long-distance transmission mileage in the country. It was also conceivable that future competitors might emerge from among fiber-optics suppliers who could expand into operations through contracting or subsidiaries.

But the new technologies produced tremendous growth in demand for communications products and services, and hesitation was the last competitive response any player would take. Between 1950 and 1972 the numbers of telephones and conversations increased 200 percent, while the number of local central offices accommodating this traffic increased 85 percent. In 1950 there were 30 million routing combinations linking central offices; by 1972 the 85 percent growth of these offices had multiplied the routing combinations nearly four times.

Telephone use had not peaked, appeared not to be limited by demographic trends, and surely would keep multiplying at geometric rates. As John Brooks writes, "Telephone use, it turns out, increases markedly faster than the square of population growth, with no leveling off in sight."[19] The field of data communications, which included not only the linking of computer systems and data bases, but also electronic funds transfer, credit card verification, and biomedical and law enforcement applications, grew even faster in the 1970s than the square of population growth. In 1972 revenues for data communications added up to less than $1 billion. By 1985, predicted revenues totaled over $20 billion.

The new technologies caught the eye of entrepreneurs in other industries; the field attracted numerous new players when consumer demand increased and the untapped markets mushroomed. Some of the largest U.S. corporations—IBM, Xerox, Exxon, RCA, and others—which traditionally served different markets from AT&T's, began to encroach on the company's territory. The financial stakes were enormous; by the mid-1970s industry revenues were pushing $40 billion domestically, and some forecasts predicted annual revenues of $250 billion by 1985. "Plain old telephone service" accounted for more than 90 percent of the present income, but the remaining business (data and facsimile transmission) was growing twice as fast as voice transmission. The market for hardware was also growing rapidly. In 1973 total expenditures for electronic equipment in the industry exceeded $12 billion and were growing at about 9 percent per annum. Figure 2–1 shows some of the new technologies and the range of possible industry competition. Technological and market pressures had combined to change the FCC's historic belief that communications was a natural monopoly.

Although MCI is generally viewed as the competitor that penetrated AT&T's monopoly, the beginnings of a market challenge can be traced to two FCC rulings in the 1950s. The Hush-a-Phone decision (1956) established for the first time that independent suppliers could sell equipment that was attached to the network without AT&T's permission, and the 1959 "Above 890" decision allowed private firms to use the radio spectrum above 890 megacycles (microwave frequencies) for transmission needs not met by existing common carriers.

Two parallel decisions of the 1960s opened the door wider. The Hush-a-Phone had not involved an electrical device, but the FCC's 1968 Carterfone decision extended the principle of permitting "for-

Horizontal Function	TERMINAL EQUIPMENT	Interconnect Market	LOCAL EXCHANGE	Specialized Common Carriers	LONG-DISTANCE EXCHANGE
New Technology	Telephones Telegraph Teletypes Electronic typewriters Data services Facsimile transmission	PBXs Key systems Advanced switching systems Office systems	CB radio Pocket page service Cable TV Mobile radio	Satellites Fiber optics	Microwave radio
Major Competition	Traditional competitors, (e.g., Automatic Electric, Northern Telecom, Stromberg-Carlson, etc.) Computer and electronics firms International competition (Europe and Japan, Taiwan)	ITT Danray Rolm Ethernet (Xerox, DEC, Intel) Exxon RCA	(Major competition in the future)	Comsat RCA America Satellite Corporation Satellite Business Systems (IBM, Aetna, Comsat) Corning, 3M, DuPont	MCI Southern Pacific Western Union ITT

Related:

Western Union ⟶
Graphnet ⟶
Telenet ⟶
Post Office ⟶

Figure 2–1. *Changing Technology and the Competitive Challenge to AT&T, 1970–1980*

eign attachments" to electrical equipment (that is, non-Bell products to be connected to the Bell network), thereby legalizing the interconnect business. The next year the commission prepared the way for competitors in long-distance services to get started by approving MCI's application to offer intercity communications for businesses via microwave. This ruling thus combined the principles of the "Above 890" and Carterfone decisions. (A chronology of regulatory policy changes is shown in table 2–1).

AT&T remained by far the dominant firm in all markets, but each year brought new challenges. The company lost some residential income to retailers selling telephones, but the competition was fiercest in the markets for business products and services.

The business market divided into two segments: the interconnect market (essentially, customer premises equipment), and long-distance services. Interconnect products took off after the 1968 Carterfone decision; within three years, rival companies had sold 1,800 PBXs, with features unavailable in Bell products. Most outside vendors' PBXs were connected to the natural monopolist's network. A 1973 AT&T internal study recognized the company's acute awareness of developing problems:

> Competitive PBX and key system losses are multiplying—a trend that shows every sign of continuing. Records of lost systems and revenues have been kept since the Carterfone Decision, and predictions of future losses have been made based on trends and other judgmental factors. Each year the forecast of losses has been alarmingly high and has evoked many expressions of disbelief. The fact is that all forecasts to date have proven to be too low. The forecast for 1973 anticipates the loss of 9,600 PBX and key systems. If the first eight months of 1973 are a good indicator, that total loss figure will be closer to 12,000.

Competition in long-distance services from specialized common carriers such as MCI and Southern Pacific posed a similar threat. Microwave companies brought in $30 million in 1972 and were growing rapidly. The revenues of satellite carriers surpassed $100 million in the mid-1970s, with predicted revenues of $2 billion by the mid-1980s.[20]

Table 2–1
Chronology of Regulatory History

1907	The first state regulatory agencies to monitor rates form in Wisconsin and New York.
1910	The Mann–Elkins Act makes the Interstate Commerce Commission (ICC) responsible for overseeing telephone companies. In 1913 the ICC establishes uniform accounting principles for reporting but does not set rates, either then or later.
1913	The Kingsbury Commitment effectively ends competition in the telephone business. The principles of the commitment were later embodied in federal legislation, the Willis–Graham Act of 1921.
1918	Telephone and telegraph service is nationalized by the government during World War I. Private control resumes in 1919.
1934	The Communications Act of 1934 shifts regulatory responsibility from the ICC to the Federal Communications Commission (FCC). Active regulation of interstate telephone rates begins.
1943	Public policy forces changes in telephone accounting procedures, requiring long-distance toll revenues to support costs of local exchanges. The effect is to encourage growth of local service.
1956	The FCC issues its Hush-a-Phone decision, authorizing an independent company to attach nonelectrical equipment to the Bell System without AT&T's permission.
1959	The FCC's "Above 890" decision permits firms to employ private microwave communications systems to meet their own needs.
1968	The FCC's Carterfone decision authorizes the connection of customer-owned electrical equipment to the telephone network.
1969	The FCC permits a private corporation to offer specialized communications services aimed at business traffic between Chicago and St. Louis.
1971	The FCC's Specialized Common Carrier (SCC) decision allows special service carriers to compete with telephone companies for "nonvital" services such as private, leased lines.
1972	The FCC's domestic satellite decision opens satellite communications to competition.

Strains on Bell System Organization

The changing nature of the telecommunications industry and regulatory policy threatened every component of the Bell System. At Bell Labs and Western Electric, the traditional pure-science methods of conducting research and development or manufacturing were becoming anachronistic in a competitive world. Moreover, the relationship between AT&T and the BOCs posed immediate problems. The combination of new technologies, rapidly increasing demand, and the beginnings of competition pointed up inadequacies in the traditional functional organization.

A series of embarrassing service crises in major metropolitan areas in the late 1960s first called AT&T's traditional strategy and structure into question by focusing attention on the inability of the functional organization to mobilize resources. The increased sophistication and complexity of the network demanded correspondingly increased levels of technical expertise and administration. Advanced technology reduced the need for operator services, thus creating an imbalance of power among the functional departments as engineering and plant eclipsed traffic. At the same time, as customer products like PBXs became more complex, so did service orders, which required more interdepartmental coordination.

Several BOCs began to modify their organizations to meet their new environments. By 1973 all BOCs either had conducted major organizational studies or were seriously contemplating such studies. The studies indicated the need for sweeping organizational restructuring, and some BOCs were already beginning to implement changes. The emerging variations in BOC structures suggested a trend toward further organizational diversity and decentralization. One danger in this trend was the growing lack of consistency throughout the System.

AT&T's internal study pointed out management problems. The increasing complexity of the business had made it extremely difficult for top managers to trace accountability in the functional structure. One BOC vice-president recounted the following scenario in a 1980 interview:

> I would meet with my subordinates, trying to identify responsibility for breakdowns in metropolitan service. The operations people claimed there was too little new plant to meet growth, the engineers pointed to traffic estimates, and the traffic engineers pointed to commercial forecasts. Although oversimplified, this scene was repeated over and over and reflects the shortcomings of the traditional structure. Even with its inherent strengths of developing expertise at higher levels and providing a check and bal-

ance system between departments, the traditional structure fragments responsibility for customer service and does not lend itself to quick responses to unusual demands.

By October 1973, the seven BOCs that still retained the traditional functional structure were beginning to restructure by creating general manager positions with responsibilities across the functions at levels below that of vice-president. Nearly half of the BOCs had formed some kind of network or switching department; five had formed customer services departments, which combined commercial, plant, and traffic functions into units centered in the flow of service orders. Several companies had split off operator services from other traffic functions as a separate department. At three companies, all functions for providing customer equipment and local routing were brought together under the heading of customer service, and various network functions were merged into a network operations department. At another company, major line functions were divided into units called network services, customer services, business services, operator services, and facilities management.

Still other companies adopted new organizational objectives. Such guidelines included decentralization of line operations, consolidation of central staff, and restructuring of organizations around the normal flow of work in order to improve interdepartmental coordination. In another variation, one company reorganized operations into two geographic regions, each subdivided into "natural task units": customer operations, network operations, and operator services.

Organizational diversity was spreading in the Bell System, and key executives were growing alarmed. At a semiannual meeting in 1970, BOC presidents placed organization structure at the top of their list of "crucial issues for the coming years." The resulting internal AT&T study discussed corporate implications:

> Several Operating Companies have reorganized to meet pressures caused by growth, technology, and competition and to more clearly delineate accountability for major segments of the business. A general pattern is becoming obvious, but a great deal of diversity still exists among these companies. Allowing indepen-

dent reorganization to continue risks increasing diversity throughout the Bell System and a consequent erosion of the unity derived
from the historical similarity of structures.

Strategic Reorientation

President Gifford's slogan that the telephone company's mission was
"to furnish the best possible service at the lowest possible cost"
served as the operational strategy of the Bell System for more than
fifty years. As a current corporate planner put it, "In the past, earnings were seen as necessary to support service, as a means rather
than an end." AT&T allocated resources and formulated strategy
based on its conception of service and a gradual cultivation of
new technology. According to the headquarters vice-president of
finance:

> Resource allocation under the old system was responsive to ser-
> vice requirements. You put resources in New York because of
> rapid growth there. You also responded to the service ethic. You
> allocated money to service and franchise requirements. It was a
> matter of engineering economics after that, weighing Case A ver-
> sus Case B. There was little risk involved. We knew we could get
> price increases from regulatory agencies to cover new expansion.

Indeed, prior to 1970, strategic planning at AT&T was essentially network planning, product design, and fund allocation for
network development and expansion. Historically, the System worried first about its capital needs, next about its expenses and only
then about its revenues. In any event, costs of products and services
were recoverable, for the regulatory agencies were responsive to adjusting the allowable rate of return. Finally, in a monopolistic environment and an expanding economy, revenues took care of
themselves.

By the early 1970s, however, AT&T's traditional strategy and
structure were no longer tenable. Two factors, the attainment of the
original goal of universal service—more than 90 percent of Ameri-
cans now had access to telephone service—and the changing regulatory and competitive environment, forced AT&T to reconsider its

ways. Accordingly, in 1973 the company's Executive Policy Committee asked the Corporate Planning Organization (CPO) to prepare a comprehensive study of Bell System structure. The CPO's mandate was "to examine existing organizational change in the Bell System, to consider technological and social forces, and to develop alternative decision options regarding AT&T and Operating Company structures."

The CPO submitted its report in October 1973. On the basis of internal interviews and external research, the CPO determined that the complex job of building integrated organizational structures could be simplified greatly by seeking answers to three fundamental organizational questions:

1. What is the best grouping of basic business activities to meet the strategic objectives of the firm?

2. At what level should general management across functions be established?

3. How can professional specialists best be deployed?

With a goal of developing distinct restructuring alternatives, three different groupings of basic activities were presented: traditional, customer/network/operator services, and competitive. These choices penetrated the heart of AT&T's traditional organization (see figure 2–2):

> Since any change in organization structure is an extremely serious and often traumatic undertaking, one must ask the question, why change at all? Hence, the continuation of the present, or traditional structure must be considered a serious choice despite the fact that several companies have reorganized and pressure for more changes exists. This is even more important in light of the high degree of performance of the traditional structure over an extended period. Thus, the first alternative—the traditional structure—should serve as a standard or baseline from which to judge the other two. The departmental breakdown—commercial, plant, traffic, engineering, and sales—is basically functional and except for minor modifications, that structure has remained intact.

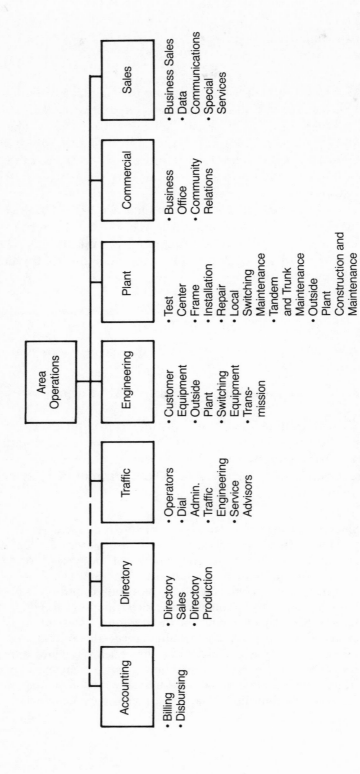

Figure 2–2. *Traditional Organization*

The second alternative grouped AT&T's products according to natural tasks rather than functional skills. Activities were clustered on the basis of work flows or processes within the company. Three large segments were planned: (1) customer service activities, based mostly on the service order flow; (2) network services, with related switching and trunk provision activities; and (3) operator services, which, though still based more on functional skills than on processes, would be separated and create only minimal interface connections with the other two segments (see figure 2–3).

Customer services included all activities needed to provide the customer with station equipment and loop connection to the central office, including business office contact and negotiation, sales activities, assignment of cable pair and terminal, and installation and repair of station equipment. Construction and supporting engineering functions (customer equipment and outside plant) would be integrated with day-to-day activities to give the customer services manager control of both the provision of the plant and its daily operations and maintenance needs. The network services grouping included all network design, engineering, and construction (Western Electric interface), as well as operation and maintenance of the network with accountability for network performance lying with one manager below the operating vice-president level. Seven of the BOCs had already reorganized and included elements of the customer/network/operators services structure. In addition, several of their internal studies had pointed toward this process-oriented structure.

The third alternative—the competitive structure—was geared to handle the competitive threats in the terminal market, while also serving as a viable alternative for meeting the growing demands and needs of business customers within the regulatory framework (see figure 2–4). Furthermore, this structure avoided possible regulatory complications by providing for an alignment of broad market segments without vertically integrating the terminal market. The competitive structure shared similarities with the customer/network/operator services structure in that operating segments of the business were again basically separated into two groupings: customer and network. Major differences included the splitting of the customer services functions into residence and business services, and the cre-

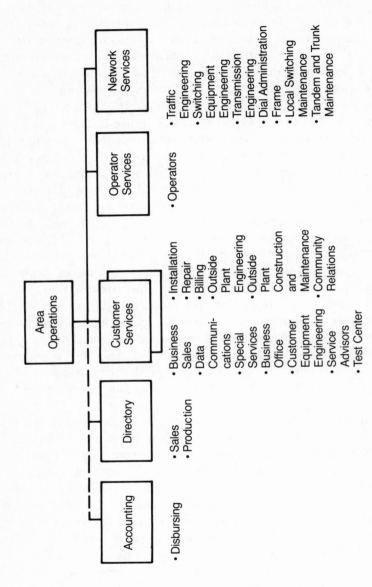

Figure 2–3. *Customer/Network/Operator Services Alternative*

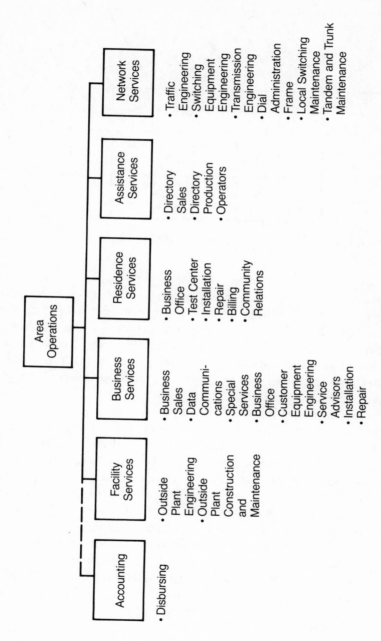

Figure 2–4. *Competitive Alternative*

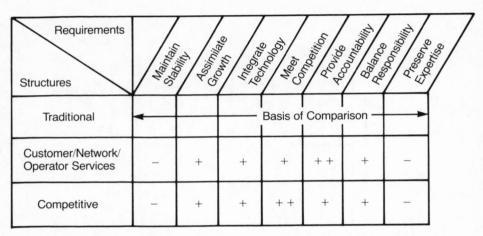

Requirements / Structures	Maintain Stability	Assimilate Growth	Integrate Technology	Meet Competition	Provide Accountability	Balance Responsibility	Preserve Expertise
Traditional	←			Basis of Comparison			→
Customer/Network/ Operator Services	–	+	+	+	+ +	+	–
Competitive	–	+	+	+ +	+	+	–

Figure 2–5. *Matching Structure to Corporate Requirements*

ation of an assistance service group (directory functions and oper-ator services). The business services group would consolidate the functions that dealt directly with business customers and would in-clude those services that supported them. Significantly, this group-ing included its own installation and repair functions and would give the unit the capability to generate an appropriate and timely response to business customers.

Residence services followed the same logic as business services: its design relied on relatively self-sufficient units. Functions were combined that interfaced with the customer in the negotiation and implementation phases of a transaction. Additionally, resident ser-vices included community relations activities, thereby integrating the complete residence customer response. All functions were under the control of a single manager at the local level.

The assistance services grouping united the directory and oper-ator services functions, and provided an organization unit geared to those customers who wanted something extra in their day-to-day use of the telephone—including operator assistance in placing calls and finding numbers. The unit's objective was to provide assistance services profitably rather than treating them as an expense that needed to be minimized.

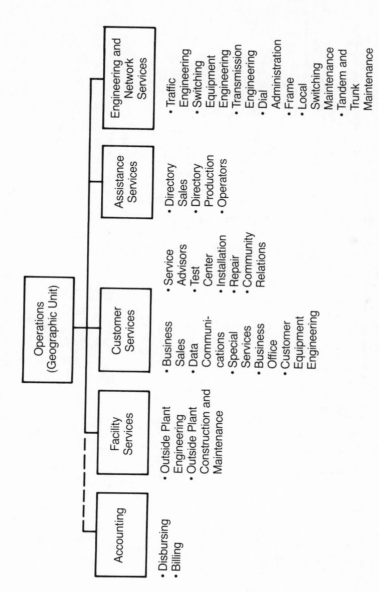

Figure 2–6. *Recommended Operating Company Structure*

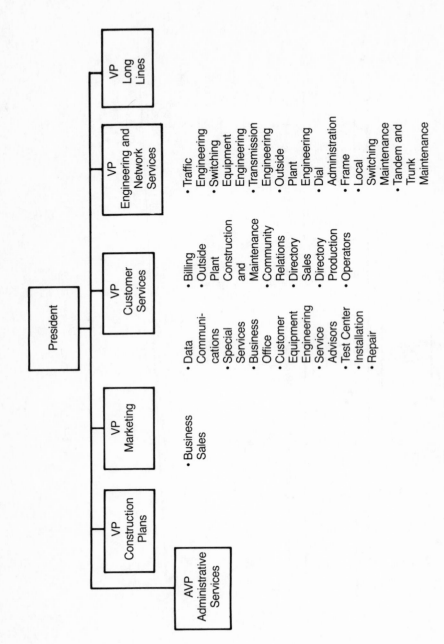

Figure 2–7. *Recommended AT&T Structure*

Choice and Implementation

The CPO analyzed the three alternatives at length. Figure 2–5 shows the organization's efforts to match recommended structure to its corporate requirements. Eventually, the CPO recommended the structure shown in Exhibit 2–6 for the BOCs and the structure shown in Exhibit 2–7 as the model for AT&T staff. The new structure, which combined features of the customer/network/operator services and the competitive models, was designed to meet the challenges of growth assimilation, technology integration, competitive threats, and controlled accountability. Restructuring decisions were announced to the BOC presidents at their November 1973 conference. The BOCs were encouraged to proceed at their own speed, as AT&T did not want to be "inconsistent with the historical license contact role of advice and counsel."

Part II
Stress

Despite the customer/network/operator services reorganization, the Bell System confronted a darkening business environment in the 1970s. Technological innovation, deregulation of particular markets, and competitive rivalry continued to pose substantial threats to System organization and operations. In response, AT&T pursued a twofold strategy. It lobbied strenuously to overturn the piecemeal advance of deregulation and simultaneously launched a major effort to improve its marketing capability to meet the new competition.

Throughout the decade, AT&T protested to no avail against competitive encroachments. The company's case boiled down to four points. First, AT&T charged that FCC orders were unfair. Bell was not permitted to compete in certain markets, such as integrated communications services, whereas its rivals could do so. Second, AT&T argued that regulatory decisions allowed its competitors to skim the cream of business, taking away the lucrative intercity business telephone traffic and leaving Bell to deliver the much costlier residential service. The company claimed that if cream skimming continued unabated, then residential rates would have to rise unilaterally, particularly in rural areas.

Third, AT&T argued that since separations and settlements policies allocated costs among the local exchanges and long-distance network, then competing long-distance companies ought to pay a "network access charge" to the Bell System to cover the costs shared by the local exchange. Finally, AT&T claimed that if competition in the industry brought savings to the public in the forms of efficiency and innovation, then it would be at the cost of public service. In a competitive environment AT&T would be far less willing and able to redistribute its work force during emergencies or to build costly backup systems into the network. As Chairman John deButts put it in testimony before the U.S. Senate in 1973:

> The service motivation has been bred in the bones of telephone people over the course of a hundred years. To supplant that motivation with a market motivation might make us a no less profitable business and a no less effective one, though by different standards. But we would be a different business surely and I, for one, cannot help but feel that we would be the poorer for it and so would the public we serve.[1]

On the marketing front, AT&T's challenge was formidable. Although the corporation had created a marketing department in 1959, the function was barely developed. After all, in a monopolistic environment, customers had little choice but to use Bell products and services. By the mid-1970s, however, the situation had changed dramatically. To upgrade Bell System marketing, deButts hired senior executives from such companies as IBM, Procter & Gamble, and Xerox, and commissioned a major consulting firm to study AT&T's sales practices. The eventual fruit of this effort was a new, comprehensive approach, the Bell Marketing System, which segmented customers by lines of business. However, AT&T's sudden shift of priorities away from traditional functions proved controversial among career employees who had hired on with what now seemed obsolete expectations.

The Bell Operating Companies, for their part, experienced frustration in interpreting corporate guidelines for reorganization and implementing the Bell Marketing System. Jack MacAllister, president of Northwestern Bell, believed that organizational problems stemmed from AT&T corporate staff's overzealous attempts to maintain centralized control. He argued that increasing competitive rivalry demanded a Bell System response in the form of greater decentralization. Thus, under his guidance, Northwestern Bell seized the opportunity to change from a militaristic style of management that demanded methods, procedures, practices, and structure to a system that pushed decision responsibility down to where the information and action were.

Chapters 3, 4, and 5 describe the efforts of AT&T and Northwestern Bell to redefine their strategies and structures in response to increasing competitive pressures. To complicate matters, these efforts occurred against a shifting political and economic background. As the 1970s closed, AT&T and BOC managers sensed that changing government attitudes toward regulation would continue to constrain their ability to manage change.

Table II–1 charts the environment and challenges facing the Bell System from 1974 to 1980, and can be used as a guide to chapters 3, 4, and 5.

Table II–1
The Bell System, 1974–1980

Industry environment:	Increasing competition. New players emerging and eroding monopoly status.
Policy environment:	Becoming uncertain.
Regulatory justification:	Natural monopoly, but emerging federal concern with pricing and innovation.
Regulatory challenge:	Technological developments challenge supremacy of technological efficiency argument.
Pressures for change:	Increasing. New product and market challenges.
Key management problems:	Reorient the company to face competitive challenges. Develop marketing capability. Manage the definition of a new strategic consensus. Reduce costs.
Internal environment and capacity for change:	Increasingly stressful. Efforts to achieve new corporate goals inhibited; productivity problems, in-house fighting, and staff anxiety increasing. Growing independence of operating companies. Adaptation in process of definition and partial implementation.

3
A New Marketing Orientation

AT&T's 1973 reorganization replaced the Bell System's traditional functional structure with a *systems* organization, in which natural tasks were grouped according to internal work flows and processes. This customer/network/operator services structure was intended primarily to help manage the operating complexities engendered by growth and more sophisticated telecommunications technology. With improved coordination and accountability for service, AT&T believed the embarrassing service crises would end. Operating performance was also expected to improve. Where the old structure had carried functional differentiation up to the very top of the managerial hierarchy, the systems organization featured integrating linkages at middle-management levels. Basic functional units were left unchanged, as was the extensive system of internal operating and service performance measures.

The pace of implementation at the BOCs was left largely to the discretion of local management, but reorganization came slowly. In 1978 some BOCs were still in the process of restructuring to the customer/network/operator services orientation.

Accelerating Change

Between 1973 and 1978, major developments occurred in the telecommunications environment. Although AT&T had anticipated some changes, others came more strongly than anticipated. Declining costs and improved performances of digital computers caused further increases in the volume of data communications; greater diversity in products and services required by customers escalated, especially in the crucial large-business user market. At the same time, decreased switching and transmission costs through the use of microwave, satellites, fiber optics, digital transmission, pocket switching, and computer-based customer premises switching equipment were gradually eroding the economies of scale on which the Bell System's regulated status was based.

The merging technology of communications and data processing revealed weaknesses in the FCC's method of defining the boundary between regulated telecommunications and unregulated data-processing businesses. Under the terms of the 1956 consent decree and the FCC's "first computer inquiry," which ended in 1971, AT&T was forbidden to enter the data-processing business, and other transmission vendors were allowed to do so only by setting up independent, arm's-length subsidiaries. In 1976, however, the FCC allowed AT&T to introduce the Dataspeed/40, a "smart" terminal that, though technically within the FCC's definition of data communication, provided local memory, text editing, and compatibility with remote computers. It was a tentative first step into data processing.

AT&T's attempt to defend its regulated-monopoly position on the basis of the need for an integrated telecommunication system and end-to-end responsibility for service encountered a number of setbacks before legislatures and regulatory and judicial bodies, leading eventually to some loss of regulatory protection. Proposed congressional legislation supporting the network concept (widely known as the "Bell bill") died in committee, and it was known that the House Subcommittee on Communications was preparing a bill aimed at promoting competition in the industry. The FCC ordered AT&T to interconnect with specialized common carriers on the same terms as its own Long Lines department; MCI was now authorized to compete in the long-distance market; and outside vendors were allowed to sell and hook up approved terminal equipment into the Bell network system. AT&T's petition supporting its "primary instrument concept" (which specified that every single-line subscriber, whether business or residential, should have at least one carrier-supplied telephone for purposes of testing, service continuity, and quality comparison) was denied. Their attempt to use the natural-monopoly argument as a competitive weapon essentially failed at the FCC. And the Justice Department filed another antitrust suit calling for divestiture of Western Electric and Bell Laboratories.

Actual and potential competition continued to increase dramatically, especially in the business market. Between 1973 and 1978 the number of terminal manufacturers and models doubled, and the annual revenues of the specialized common carriers increased 200-fold, from less than $1 million to over $200 million. In the early 1970s, most competitors were undercapitalized entrepreneurs; by 1978, however, the list of potential entrants included ITT in the specialized common carrier business, IBM in the domestic satellite market, and Xerox and GTE in network service.

Beyond Customer Service

Although AT&T continued to fight open entry into the telecommunications industry, it also readied itself to compete in a new environment. After the Carterfone decision, annual reports stressed that "should competition be authorized, the Bell System will prove itself an aggressive and effective competitor" (1970). When John deButts became chairman in 1972, he took office firmly committed to changing the company's strategic focus: "With competition coming, it was pretty obvious that we had to become more market oriented."[2]

Early in deButts's tenure, AT&T hired a major consulting firm to analyze its sales organization. Some of the results pointed out that sales personnel spent only 30 percent of their time actually selling; moreover, it was plausible (indeed, it was a common experience) that sales representatives were responsible for two functions that occasionally competed with each other: selling and customer service. The Bell System's traditional emphasis on quality of service meant that selling often took a back seat to workable solutions that used existing services and equipment. Under the traditional guidelines, it was more appropriate to satisfy than to sell, and representatives worked toward achieving lower repair bills rather than a higher sales volume.

On receipt of the consulting firm's report, AT&T experimented with a change in its local sales organization; it provided sales reps with assistants who supervised postorder activity. The results showed that the new approach increased actual selling time significantly. Another AT&T study revealed that 52 percent of the customers who bought competitors' products and services had not even been contacted by a Bell representative. After Bell added the sales assistants to the test sites, sales losses to the independents dropped to 17 percent. Still, even after implementation of the new sales organization, over three-quarters of sales personnel had combined sales and service responsibilities in 1975.[3]

Regulation hampered these marketing efforts. New products could not be introduced into the market until regulators had approved them. When AT&T wanted to introduce its "Snoopy" phone, it had to go to fifty-four different regulatory bodies for approval. Since all rate filings were public, potential competitors had ample time to examine AT&T's proposals and devise appropriate responses to steal new markets away.

As problems became more evident, deButts ordered changes in the marketing department and put Kenneth Whalen, former president of Michigan Bell, at the helm. Whalen's job was to set up the first coordinated marketing effort in the company's history. The magnitude of his task was well understood and acknowledged; nobody in the company really knew what marketing management was. With the chairman's backing, outsiders were hired from firms with national reputations in marketing (including IBM, Procter & Gamble, and Xerox) and were placed in key supportive positions.

With a liberal budget and ample time, the marketing department started up. Once established, it consisted of some seven hundred people drawn almost equally from inside and outside the Bell System. The key executive in the new department was Arch McGill, a former vice-president at IBM and consultant to high-technology firms who joined AT&T in 1973 as head of market management. Drawing on his own training, the consultant's report, and his own perception of the telephone business, McGill attempted to force the Bell System to reevaluate its fundamental attitudes. Recalling his first days with the company, McGill said:

> From the outset I understood the crucial issues [of the telephone business] and coming in I laid down a very strict set of criteria which I knew had to be met in order for me to make the job

work. . . . The key elements I negotiated were the freedom to hire outside; an unlimited budget; and no time limits on producing quick results. I knew it would take time to turn this organization around.

With responsibility for the entire marketing mix, including business and residence, McGill began to study and design the marketing program. At the same time, he began auditing program and services development from his aggressive marketing perspective.

When I first came in 1973, I asked a lot of people about what they meant by "The best possible service at the lowest possible cost." Everybody had a different answer, right up to the chairman. The reason was that no one really knew what our customers wanted, what service meant to them. There was no sense of how our products fulfilled our customers' communication needs, which is my definition of the business we're in.

McGill and his staff spent their first three years getting to understand AT&T's customer base, as market segmentation became the key issue facing the mammoth corporation:

At the top level, I divided the market into four parts: Business, Residence, Directory, and Public [pay phones]. Five years later that became the basis of the whole organizational structure. Since Business had the greatest potential and the highest risk, that's where I spent most of our time. Within Business, I decided to segment along industry lines. Others wanted to segment by type of usage or by size of customer. But that doesn't help you understand the customer's business, which is the only thing that really makes a difference. The idea was to figure out where the customer can displace costs or add value by buying telecommunication equipment and services.

Once the customer needs analysis was completed, McGill then worked on AT&T's lines of products and services.

Our thrust areas were identified as data processing, energy management, and telecommunications applications like teleconferencing. In the Business segment we'll totally displace our current line by 1985. That kind of turnover is new for the Bell System. In the past it's been only about five to ten percent every five years. Bell executives are always screaming about the sunk costs in existing plant. But you have to move.

The Bell Marketing System

During the mid-1970s, McGill also helped develop and introduce the Bell Marketing System, (BMS), an interrelated set of marketing concepts, job designs, organizational structures, commitment processes, performance measures, incentives, and career paths (see figures 3–1 and 3–2). Patterned on IBM's approach to marketing, BMS was designed to unify responsibility for each account under a

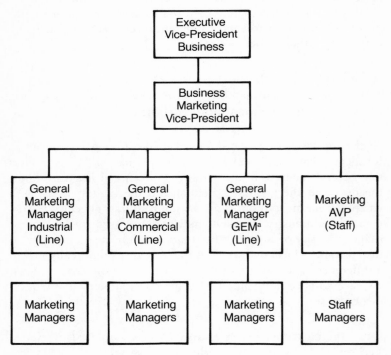

[a]Government, education, and medical.

Figure 3–1. *Bell Marketing System: Operating Company Marketing Organization*

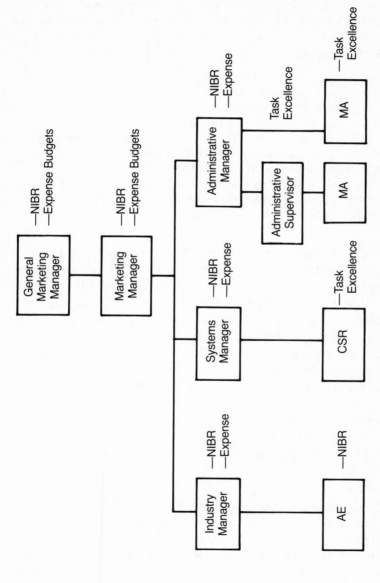

Notes: AE = account executive; CSR = communications systems representative;
MA = market administrator; NIBR = net incremental billed revenue.

Figure 3–2. *Bell Marketing System: Marketing Team and Measurements*

team of industry specialists capable of understanding a business customer's needs and designing a complete communications system for their individual satisfaction. Employee performance measures were derived by increases in the net incremental billed revenue and thus became the basis for incentive compensation.[4] As McGill described BMS's purpose:

> We want to transform our marketing effort into a proactive, positive force for change. We want to be perceived by the customer as problem-solving, not part of the problem. We want to be on the leading edge of the customer's decision processes. But that means reorienting the fundamental value system of the corporation. It's a problem not of creating dedication but of channeling it to serving specific customer needs with flexible products and services. That's not just a problem for marketing people. No part of the Bell System will remain untouched.

The BMS created a variety of new marketing, sales, and service positions. Account executives assumed primary responsibility for revenue generation; they now had total accountability for customers within their assigned market segments. Developing integrated revenue plans for each market, they were responsible for identifying goals and mobilizing resources to meet customers' needs and demands. Account executives directed customer activity, including the authority to direct, redirect, and terminate the activities of support team members who came into conflict with the realization of the account objectives established by the account executive for all assigned accounts. The thrust of the account executive's efforts was toward the sale of communications systems solutions that solved customers' business problems and contributed financially to the corporation.

Communications systems representatives' (CSRs') responsibilities occupied several position levels depending on the degree of skill and experience required. The CSR was primarily a professional technical expert, but McGill deemed his or her prime responsibility to be acting as the customer's business communications "problem solver." It was the CSR's responsibility to provide technical support for the marketing team in the areas of systems analysis, systems design, and network and market simulation, through pre- and post-sale assistance to the account executive.

Market administrators (MAs) were divided into two areas. The MA–demand had responsibility for managing customer-initiated requests and ensuring complete customer satisfaction through timely delivery of required systems. Key responsibilities included the implementation of standard voice or data communications sales, selling activities designed to upgrade or modify installed systems, and the management of business customer requests beyond the scope of the Business Service Center. The MA–voice/data was to ensure complete customer satisfaction through timely delivery of required systems, primarily complex voice and/or data applications. Key responsibilities included implementing voice or data communications systems sales, selling activities designed to upgrade or modify installed systems, and handling assigned customer-initiated requests beyond the scope of the MA–demand role.

Service representatives were an integral part of the marketing team as they managed incoming customer requests and responded to customer inquiries. Often acting as the first line of contact for most small businesses, they also handled larger accounts when routine telecommunication changes were required. It was essential that they performed their functions fully in order that upper management could carry out their complete responsibilities.

A Second Reorganization

With continued environmental change and increased emphasis on marketing, weaknesses in the 1973 customer/network/operator services organization were becoming exposed. The systems structure still emphasized functional skills on a basis of differentiation and, despite McGill's efforts, occurred at the expense of a market orientation. The corporate value system remained internally focused; performance measures continued to be based on technical concepts of service quality. Decision processes were slow, fragmented and bound by rigid practices and procedures. There was a tendency for network and service people to relegate marketing to the marketing department, rather than perceiving any applications that a marketing orientation might have to their work.

In February 1978 management sought a more pervasive change that would extend beyond merely rearranging work functions. John deButts, retiring as chairman of the board, announced that the Bell System would reorganize once again. The task force appointed to coordinate the change was directed by Kenneth Whalen, who was to become the new executive vice-president–residence, and Thomas E. Bolger, who was to be the executive vice-president–business. The task force included two executives representing each of the business, residence, and network segments, and Brooke Tunstall, director of corporate planning, who provided staff support. McGill was one of the business representatives. The task force also selected one multistate and one single-state operating company to participate in the planning.

The task force emerged with the basic structure shown in figure 3–3 and was eventually implemented in the form shown in figure 3–4. Commenting on the new structure, the new AT&T chairman, Charles L. Brown, observed:

> With some translation, the boxes on the organization chart of the new structure can be seen not only as slots to be filled but as tools for realizing our strategic priorities.
>
> The top level of the chart—three segments representing business, residence, and network—shows the aspect of reorganization already most familiar to most managers. The separation of business and residence allows for a direct emphasis on the separate needs of business and residence customers. The network, redefined as "from protector to protector," can be maintained as a resource for both market segments. Accountability for all operations is located within each segment.
>
> Organization by markets has another advantage: it allows for subsegmentation where and when the nature of the markets and the operating conditions make that desirable. This means greater flexibility in responding to changing markets and needs. The formation of directory and public communications units within the residence segment at AT&T are an example of such segmentation.
>
> What about service objectives? The chart makes it clear how those objectives are protected. Within each major market segment, some units concentrate their attention upon marketing goals, others upon service goals. Units emphasizing marketing are

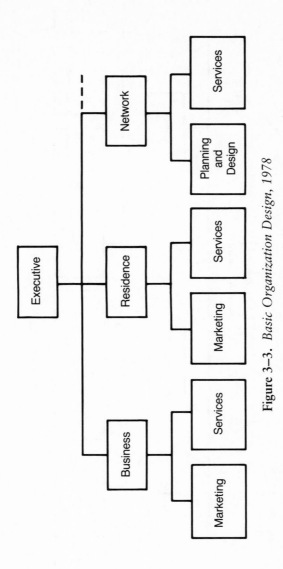

Figure 3–3. *Basic Organization Design, 1978*

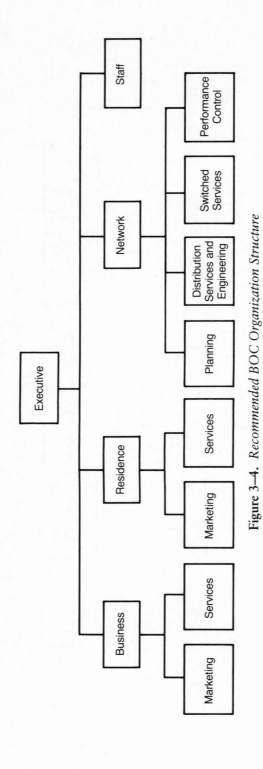

Figure 3–4. *Recommended BOC Organization Structure*

responsible for all functions up to delivery of the service, including price determination, forecasting, product management, and sales; units responsible for service handle all functions from the point of delivery of service, such as installation, repair, maintenance, and training.

The objective of futurity—responsiveness to long-term trends—also is built into the structure. Within segments, strategic and tactical tasks often are separated; this separation allows us to keep a managerial eye both on day-to-day operations and long-term issues. With such strategy/tactics split vision, we can function well in the present while we concurrently prepare for, and influence, the future.

In addition to recommending the basic structure, the task force developed guidelines for the operating companies, and each BOC was asked to submit its implementation plan and timetable to AT&T corporate headquarters by October 15, 1978. In contrast to the 1973 reorganization, which was implemented over a five-year period, there was considerable pressure to move quickly; 1979 was to be the transition year for changing to the market-oriented structure.

By the end of 1978, many recognized that the task of reorganization had just begun. Challenges that had been handled somewhat amorphously for years were suddenly seeping in through the organization's weak spots. Commenting on the magnitude of the change, Brown said:

There is an Old Chinese saying: "May you live in interesting times." We in the Bell System live in interesting times. The current structural changes are not the first in Bell System history, but they are probably the most far reaching. They are a response to equally far reaching changes in the society we serve. And we can expect the pace of change—organizational and social—to accelerate.

Yet we also can be confident that, for some years to come, we will not witness another restructuring of this magnitude. Our new structure will flourish through gradual and continuing smaller transformations. We have tried to build flexibility into the organizational form itself. The ability to identify and adapt to changing conditions is a primary feature of our corporate structure.

4

Managing Change at Northwestern Bell: Part I

In 1978, the idea of a market segment organization was not a new one for the Bell System. Five years earlier, AT&T had recognized the need to change its traditional functional structure and had considered adopting an organization composed of several market-oriented units with a network unit operating as a common resource. At that time, however, the Bell System was heavily committed to preserving its historic role as a regulated monopoly. By 1978, however, it was clear that trends toward deregulation and competition were continuing, particularly in the business communications market. Most observers read AT&T's decision to adopt a market segment organization as a response to competitive pressures in business markets.

The problem for the Bell System as a whole was to translate the basic concept of the new organization into a working structure of job responsibilities, reporting relationships, decision processes, management systems, and career paths. A key part of this problem was managing the organization design and implementation process in the Bell System's twenty-three operating companies. Although most of these companies were wholly owned by AT&T, their managers enjoyed considerable autonomy in managing the marketing and delivery of telephone service in their respective regions. During the 1970s many had planned or implemented their own organizational changes in response to the same environmental forces that were behind AT&T's decision to reorganize the entire Bell System.

It was clear that the success of the new reorganization would depend significantly on how the operating companies carried it out.

One operating company actively involved in the planning for reorganization was the Northwestern Bell Telephone Company, whose territory included Minnesota, Iowa, North Dakota, and Nebraska. Like many multistate BOCs, Northwestern Bell's traditional organization divided the company into several state organizations, each headed by a vice-president (state CEO). Northwestern Bell's five state CEOs reported to an operating vice-president at corporate headquarters in Omaha, who in turn reported to the president. Each state CEO had line authority over the functional departments within his territory. Northwestern Bell's territories included Minnesota, Iowa, North Dakota, South Dakota, and Nebraska.

By late 1977, Northwestern Bell had largely completed the 1973 transition from the traditional structure based on plant, traffic, commercial, engineering, and sales functions to the customer/network/operator services grouping. Although the change involved considerable rearrangement of middle management's functional responsibilities, it had little effect on top management, who continued to emphasize the line authority and responsibility of the state CEO for all functions, including marketing. However, Northwestern Bell's president, Jack MacAllister, became convinced that further changes were necessary and took steps to better integrate marketing functions:

> I saw early on that the nature of our business was changing, that it was becoming more competitive, and that we had to gear our organization and people to the new environment. By early 1978, I had developed a plan for a "straight-line" marketing approach that would take responsibility for marketing and sales out of the state organization and put it under a company-wide vice president for marketing at Northwestern Bell's corporate headquarters in Omaha. I took our plan to AT&T. Their response was, "How about going the next step and getting the whole organization focused on marketing?"

Working with Northwestern Bell and New Jersey Bell (the trial single-state BOC), the AT&T headquarters task force developed the market segment organization design; management approved it and presented it to the BOC presidents in May 1978. As expected, the plan featured the four market-oriented units (business, residence, directory, and public services) and the network organization, which served as the common centralized resource base. Over the next three months, specific BOC guidelines were formulated; the reorganization plans and timetables were due to headquarters in October.

With input from the BOC presidents, AT&T's final, BOC market-segmented guidelines were issued in September 1978. Although these were precise, interpretation and application were left to the twenty-three BOC presidents.

Implementing Change

The difficulties of implementation and compliance caused many disagreements between AT&T and the BOC presidents. At headquarters, Chairman deButts backed off a bit. A senior BOC officer quoted deButts as saying, in effect:

> AT&T's general departments are going to reorganize along market segment lines, and we need to have one person for each segment in each operating company to interface with. But the operating companies' presidents are the backbone of the Bell System, so we'll listen to you about the details.

Corporate communication was difficult. At AT&T, Brooke Tunstall said that:

> Our job was to persuade the operating companies to move closer to the guidelines. But not all the guidelines were met. Some companies initially combined the Residence and Network segments. Some kept budgeting, pricing and forecasting on a centralized basis instead of decentralizing them to the segments. In other cases, Network planning and staff functions were left in state or area organizations. But I'd say we got about 75% to 85% conformance with the guidelines.

According to Tunstall, Chairman deButts's attitude was: "If a company is meeting its services and earnings goals, I will not badger them about organizational details. But I do want one person in each BOC responsible for each segment on a companywide basis."

Some BOC managers interpreted deButts's flexible policy on compliance in political terms. One senior BOC manager said:

> Charlie Brown [then president of AT&T] was rumored to be the architect of the reorganization, and some of the BOC presidents thought it was his big power play. He was president at the time, but we didn't know whether he, Jim Olson, or Bill Ellinghaus would succeed deButts. The old entrenched Bell System operating presidents all lined up to figure out how to torpedo the reorganization and Charlie Brown.
>
> Looking back, I think deButts had already picked Charlie Brown as the next chairman, and the two of them decided to get the organization set up the way Brown wanted before deButts retired. But deButts was too much of a traditionalist to pressure the BOC presidents into doing something they didn't want to do.

Others pointed out that AT&T's flexible attitude toward compliance with the guidelines was consistent with the parent company's traditional "license and advise" relationship with the operating companies, and MacAllister commented:

> In general, AT&T does give an operating company president fairly good latitude in running the company. The contacts between the two are fairly infrequent. I presume if your earnings or service program is very weak or if you've seriously deviated from policy, there would be ample reason to talk to an operating company president. If not, there are more contacts on the staff level, with people getting procedures explained to them, than on my level.

Operating company officials, however, were concerned that the new organization would affect their traditional positive relationships with AT&T. The problems of centralized management planning and reporting relationships had some BOCs questioning just what a direct-line relationship was:

I think some of the segment vice-presidents at AT&T want straight-line [i.e., direct] reporting to them, and never mind the operating company. We're getting more and more of these "strong recommendation" letters from Whalen, executive vice-president–residence, Bolger, executive vice-president–business, and McGill. "Strong recommendation" means "we own you, do it." Sometimes they even bypass the BOC president. They want to run things on a centralized basis, and they're getting more and more obtrusive about it. Frankly, I don't think centralization is worth a damn. AT&T has 13,000 people up there in the general departments, and they need about 100. The rest contribute mainly to overhead. We're staff-heavy now, and you don't fix that by centralization.

The trend toward centralization repeated itself in the growth of national account management at AT&T. Traditionally, the responsibility for providing telephone service to large national and international business corporations rested with the various operating telephone companies, which were individually credited with the revenues generated within their territories. Responsibility for coordinating marketing and service relations was given to the BOC in whose area the customer's corporate headquarters was located. In the early 1960s, the Bell System decided these customers could be better served by a national account team within the centralized Long Lines department, and by 1977, 112 national account teams were in existence, each serving a single large customer. The number of teams grew to 150 in 1978, and 50 to 75 accounts were added in each of the following years. The trend continued and the AT&T marketing department talked about selecting up to 1,500 multistate corporate customers for national account management. Yet, each time a national account team was created, all the billed revenues and direct selling expenses from that account were transferred out of the operating telephone companies and into Long Lines. Nevertheless, the BOC marketing and service personnel were expected to give top priority to serving the regional and local needs of these customers under the direction of the national account manager.

The BOC presidents viewed the shift of responsibility, revenues, and influence to AT&T corporate headquarters with mixed feelings. Although the targeted approach helped confront competitors' marketing tactics, MacAllister pointed out the costs and chances AT&T took with such a centralized approach to regional markets:

> There's no question that national and worldwide customers need national and worldwide marketing coordination. But there are still lots of regional customers. Some people think that the way to compete is to draw all the power and control to the center. But then you lose contact with the market. You can't run the system from some corporate enclave in New Jersey. [AT&T had opened its large new corporate headquarters complex in Basking Ridge, New Jersey, in 1975.] It's essential to push the decision making down as close to the customer or the operating problem as possible. The closer you get to the AT&T board room, the farther you are from the customer.

Internal Issues

In addition to their concerns about the relationship between the BOCs and AT&T, the operating company presidents were worried about the effects of internal restructuring. John Howard, Northwestern Bell's state CEO for Minnesota in 1978, reflected on restructuring's impacts on internal organization and management:

> The reorganization plan proposed by AT&T had more turf kinds of impacts than moving us into a competitive environment. The traumatic part comes from the fact that we're a multistate company. The state CEO really ran the operation. He was either the hero or the guy in trouble. Line operations was always where the action was. The staff people at headquarters lined up between the AT&T general staff and the state people. But nothing much was happening at the staff level. The states really ran the show. We even used names like "the Minnesota Telephone Company."
>
> In my own career I've always wanted to be a line operator. I grew up with the goal of becoming a state CEO. Everyone here at corporate headquarters has come up through the ranks as a state manager. The new structure left the whole organization wondering where the new power base was going to be. Who was going to be the new boss?

Howard was concerned enough about the impact of the reorganization that he lobbied MacAllister to appoint a state CEO to the Northwestern Bell task force that was drafting the company's implementation plan. Recalling his experience, Howard said:

> Actually, I invited myself onto that task force. I felt they weren't going to have a state CEO on it because they thought we would all be biased against the idea of market segment organization. But I convinced them they needed a state CEO viewpoint up front. As it turned out, I was a lonesome voice on that committee. I was like Tiny Archibald going one-on-one with Wilt Chamberlain.

The Northwestern Bell task force considered two options for restructuring: transition planning with market segments under the state CEO or a straight-line structure by market segments. Financial accountability and budget control prevailed under the first option, and with the new emphasis on costs and a competitive structure, the option was appealing. Howard pointed out that under the previous customer/network/operator services reorganization with state control, revenue streams were better controlled and few jobs were eliminated. The straight-line market segment structure shifted control from the states to the central staff, while the structure implanted a better standardization of procedures across the states at the cost of regional diversification. Howard opposed this option but finally relented, saying, "I thought if we're going to have another trauma, let's get it over with."

Howard's reservations about the single-step reorganization partly reflected concerns about work force:

> What I was afraid would happen did happen as far as people are concerned. We cut over to the new organization in October 1978, and wound up worrying about whether there was a box for everyone rather than worrying about whether there were the right number of boxes. We wound up with a hell of a bulge. We put out the new organization chart in December 1978 in the company newspaper. There were 22 new district managers, 117 new managers, all staff people and market managers. Many objected to this, saying, "If we've got the same amount of work, why do we need more

people?" But if we hadn't done this, it would have taken four or five months longer, and everything would have ground to a halt. As it was, service didn't miss a beat, but we lost our budget control. We had no historical cost for the new segments.

I was running Minnesota at that time. My empire was being torn apart; I felt like I'd held the knife at my own surgery. I couldn't imagine what the new organization would be like. People were saying it was going to be a terrible mess. It felt like no one would be in charge, like staff people would be running the company. It completely destroyed the comfort factor in the states. A state person could always go to his state CEO for protection against corporate headquarters staff. But no longer. The people in corporate headquarters were elated. Their attitude was, for twenty years we've been bowing down to those miserable bastards in the states. Now we're on top.

Northwestern Bell's New Structure

The organization ultimately adopted by Northwestern Bell called for a modified matrix that balanced segment responsibility for marketing and delivery of service against state responsibility for financial performance, regulatory affairs, and community relations. Four senior vice-presidents reported to the president—one each for the business, residence, and network segments, and one for finance (the latter's responsibilities also included management of centralized support services).

The business and network segments were organized on a straight-line basis, with heads of functional units reporting directly to their respective senior vice-president at corporate headquarters in Omaha, with only "dotted line" reporting to state CEOs. The residence segment retained the traditional geographically oriented structure below the senior vice-president level, with all middle- and lower-level residence segment managers reporting directly to a state CEO. Figure 4–1, 4–2, and 4–3 show Northwestern Bell's top management organization before, during, and a year and a half after the transition.

In March 1979 Northwestern Bell abolished the title of operating vice-president, and Howard was given the title of senior vice-

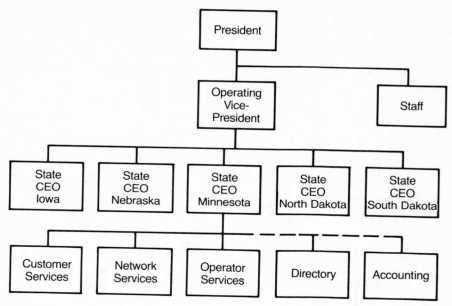

Source: Courtesy of U S WEST, Inc.

Figure 4–1. *Northwestern Bell: Traditional Structure*

president–Residence. MacAllister noted other BOCs' response to his actions:

> Some of the other operating companies were affronted because we did away with the operating vice-president position. This had been a key job, the number two man, the president's right hand. It was a position that a lot of line operating people aspired to. Most of the operating companies kept it, even though the guidelines recommended that the segment heads report directly to the president.

In addition to its basic structure, Northwestern Bell relied on a series of committees and teams for interunit coordination. The top team, the Executive Council, was responsible for resolving high-priority planning, budgeting, and operating issues, and for managing the ongoing development of organization structure and decision-making processes. The members of the Executive Council in-

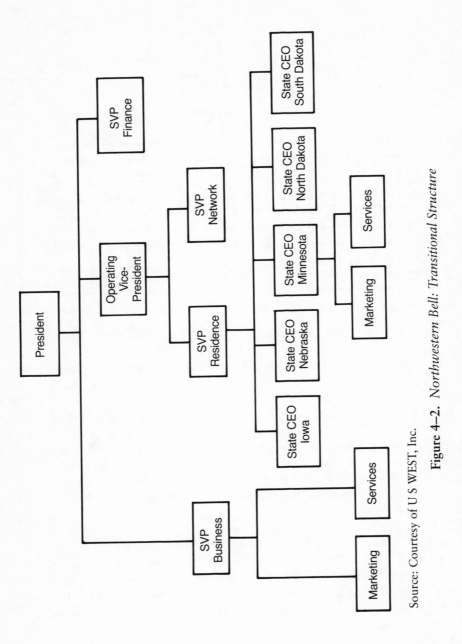

Source: Courtesy of U S WEST, Inc.

Figure 4–2. *Northwestern Bell: Transitional Structure*

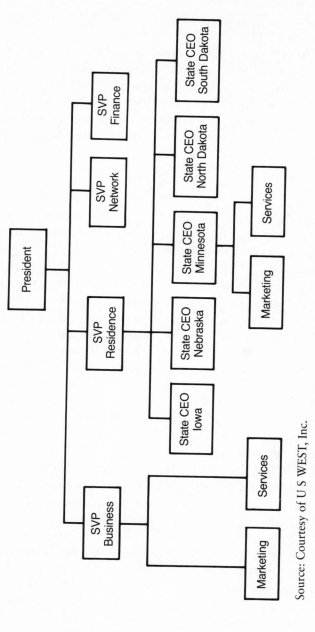

Figure 4–3. *Northwestern Bell: Market-Oriented Structure*

Source: Courtesy of U S WEST, Inc.

cluded the four senior vice-presidents; the vice-presidents for personnel, public relations and legal, and states' interests were represented by John Howard.

Five state teams were also created. Each was responsible for resolving planning, budgeting, and operating issues within its state, and for developing appropriate cross-segment and cross-functional teams wherever needed. The state teams were chaired by the state CEOs and comprised representatives from business and network functions as well as managers from the state residence organizations.

Other BOCs

Northwestern Bell's new structure was more complex than those developed at other operating companies.[5] At Mountain Bell, most of the management responsibility remained with the states, and only the marketing unit (business segment) had a straight-line organization, with marketing personnel reporting directly to companywide segment executives. All other managers in the business segment (including those responsible for service functions such as installation and repair) and the residence and network managers reported directly to a state CEO and had only dotted-line responsibilities to segment vice-presidents at company headquarters. Mountain Bell's "states' rights" approach was attributed to its geographic dispersion (it covered an area running from the Canadian to the Mexican border) and to its rapid growth, which increased demands for the expansion of basic services (local and regional market planning) and reduced pressures on earnings.

Conversely, New England Telephone organized its business, residence, and network segments on a straight-line, companywide basis. State budgets were set at corporate headquarters and allocated accordingly. State managers had only general manager rank (in other BOCs the state manager was usually a vice-president). Factors leading to this structure included a geographically compact region dominated by a single state that produced 70 percent of the company's revenues; adversarial attitudes on the part of state regulators, which reduced the importance of state managers in obtaining rate increases; and a low-growth market environment.

In South Central Bell, the state vice-presidents did not have direct-line responsibility for business, residence, or network functions, but were designated the overall coordinators for state budgets (which were constructed at the state level) and maintained responsibility for earnings, regulatory affairs, and community relations. State vice-presidents reported to a senior vice-president–finance. Segment managers had line responsibility for marketing and service but were not permitted to transfer resources freely among the states without state CEO approval. As in Northwestern Bell, a system of committees and decision processes helped manage the segment–state relationship. South Central had a relatively even distribution of revenues among the states, and its regulatory relationships appeared to be more significant at the state level than at the company level.

Management Control in the New Structure

None of the operating companies established segment profit centers. Howard commented on this situation:

> AT&T has had to back off from their initial direction. They felt we would be able to operate with paper separation between the segments, with a separate profit and loss statement for each. The idea was to use transfer charges internally. But you cannot use the profit center concept with the segments. You can't split the investment. Network has 80 percent of the resources, and if you gave them the long-distance revenues they'd generate 120 percent of the profits. So how can you run the segments as profit centers? You've got to have the people who spend the money held accountable. We want to have as much autonomy between segments as possible. You can't run the company by committee.

At Northwestern Bell, resource allocation and financial control were based on a complex process of negotiation among segment, state, and corporate staff officers. Segment units were handled as revenue and cost centers. During the budget process, each segment was responsible for estimating revenues, expenses and capital expenditures as appropriate. Revenue estimates by the business and residence segments were influenced by targets for net incremental billed revenue established by AT&T. The segment estimates were broken down by the segment managers on a state-by-state basis, and turned in to the corporate finance organization. From these, the finance staff compiled proposed budgets and pro forma profit and loss statements for each state.

On the basis of general economic trends and earnings targets set through negotiations with AT&T, the president and the Executive Council also set earnings targets for each state. Under the new organization, it was the responsibility of the state CEOs to work with segment managers within their states and at corporate headquarters to resolve the inevitable gap between proposed and expected contributions. Since only residence segment managers reported directly to the state CEOs, this process required state CEOs to take responsibility for the financial impact of business and network operations on state earnings without having direct authority over them.

The process of learning to allocate resources in the new matrix structure was complicated by the national economic slowdown that began during 1979, which created revenue shortfalls in South Dakota and Minnesota. Regulators in Iowa ordered the repayment of $40 million in charges already collected, and an unfavorable regulatory decision in California led AT&T to seek greater earnings from all the operating companies, including Northwestern Bell. The problems led to the imposition of a general personnel freeze and proportional budget cutting.

Learning to Manage in the New Structure

By late 1980, Northwestern Bell had made progress in developing the ability to manage using the new organizational structure. Several managers noted that if surplus funds were available in the old budgeting process, they tended to be allocated to the states currently earning the highest rate of return, regardless of the potential for additional earnings. As a result of interplay between segments and states, the new operations directed that allocated funds went to business units within the market with the strongest earnings potential.

This interplay meant that in Minnesota a newly created budget committee had a clear mandate to resolve conflicting state and segment budget pressures. Improvements in decision making were also apparent in marketing and operations. In Iowa and the western region (North Dakota, South Dakota, and Nebraska), marketing managers were able to work with their state CEOs and get attention for the need to develop specialized switching equipment for individual markets.

As for operations, the network segment had rearranged its preventive maintenance schedule according to need and customer impact; under the old structure this work had rotated sequentially among states. Several managers also reported that Northwestern Bell's response to flooding in North Dakota and western Minnesota was organized more rapidly because negotiations among state CEOs were unnecessary; network segment managers simply ordered the necessary work crews from three states to the affected area.

Despite the new efficiencies, significant problems remained. Because state CEOs had the primary responsibility for resolving conflicts over funding priorities and faced differing regulatory environments, the resource allocation process sometimes resulted in variation in segment spending levels across the states. With variations considered inconsistent from the corporate segment managers' viewpoint, budget disputes occasionally went unresolved.

Difficulties emerged with decision making under the new organization. Problems were often pushed up out of the states to high-level segment managers (often the senior vice-president) for resolution. These included not only budget issues involving segment managers and state CEOs, but also such questions as whether residence installation and repair personnel or network personnel would repair and test certain drop wires (the wires leading from the telephone pole to the house), and whether residence personnel in certain business service offices would answer telephones for business segment personnel located in the same office.

One manager remarked:

> The immediate effect of the reorganization was to wipe out all the communication channels we had built up over the years. People don't know who to call. Even worse, it wiped out all the prece-

dents. In the past, we had a whole body of "case law" on who was responsible for what. With the restructuring, no one knew. So a lot of problems that used to be resolved at lower levels were pushed up to the top. In many cases, the problem itself was minor; the real issue was turf.

Strategic Management

As became all too clear, preoccupation with organizational problems had diverted much attention from key strategic planning issues. As John Howard put it: "We're segmented down to a gnat's eye. But where are the opportunities?" One observer noted that decisions with strategic impact were sometimes being made on an ad hoc basis. For example, a recurrent question in marketing was whether to stay with the older Centrex system or to sell newer customer premises switching equipment such as the Dimension series PBXs. Business marketing people in Northwestern Bell and at AT&T were committed to a "product migration strategy" that aimed to maximize sales; installation of newer equipment carried a special incentive payout for marketing managers and account executives. The strategy was designed to build Bell's market position in the competitive terminal equipment business. But Dick McCormick, Northwestern Bell's senior vice-president–network, was worried about moving too fast in this direction, and took a broader look at risks and costs:

> We've already got our central offices built; the copper's in the ground. Much of it isn't depreciated yet. If we're too successful in selling customer premise equipment, we risk stranding Centrex capacity in the central office and local loop. Some operating companies have enough growth in other areas to take up the slack. In our environment, the risk is greater. We don't want to wind up cannibalizing the network.

A related concern was the relationship between capital resource allocation and strategic planning. John Howard said:

> It became very obvious last year that the Bell System had too many high-priority items. We couldn't say "no" to a good idea,

and wound up in conflict with the financial realities. There are real capital constraints for moving aggressively into new areas. If you could get [it] into the rate base, you made the investment and then went to the regulatory commission for a fair rate of return. But you can't go to the regulators for rates to justify new investment needed because of future competition. I've been hassling people to downsize our management staff since I got here. But we need a better process for setting consistent priorities. The planning process we've got doesn't drive the financial decision.

Howard Doerr, Northwestern Bell's senior vice-president–finance, agreed with Howard and expanded on the longer-term management issues facing the company:

Planning and capital resource allocation are the areas of greatest concern for us now. We need to take a more objective, independent look at capital expenditures, to analyze payback and risk. We're also concerned about follow-up and tracking—does the ROR [rate of return] achieved live up to the plan? We've hired a consultant to look at our strategic planning, but what we need and don't have right now is an S.O.B. with a long memory to run the planning and resource allocation process. It takes muscle.

Our debt ratio is up to 43 percent, and AT&T's vice-chairman and chief financial officer has told us that we've got to reduce our reliance on outside funds. There's a tremendous education job to be done. The old idea was, "If we can earn on it, get it into the rate base." In the past, we controlled the rate of introduction of new technology, so we could afford to spread out capital recovery over forty years. And we gave quality service till it wouldn't stop. The system is full of redundancies. In a competitive environment, we have learned to check whether that kind of thing is really in the best interests of the public and ourselves. That's going to mean increased emphasis on financial and analytic skills for all our managers.

5
Developing a New Culture

Transforming Northwestern Bell from an easygoing bureau-cratic organization into a forward-thinking, entrepreneurial company presented top management with a host of problems. New corporate goals and values somehow had to permeate the ranks. Employees had to learn to live with enlarged responsibilities, new paths of reporting, and new ways of relating to one another. The company had suddenly to scrutinize its cost structure and take steps to cut overhead. Marketing skills scarcely needed for most of Northwestern Bell's history now had to be acquired and applied swiftly. The pace of change had to accelerate.

The need to develop new skills was a common theme among Northwestern Bell's managers, although different executives fo-cused on different needs. Commenting on some of the difficulties with the new organization structure, Jean Smith, the vice-president for personnel, said:

> There was an immense amount of frustration in the beginning, mainly because most people did not have the skills required. We were used to a structure where the state CEOs had been nearly all-powerful, where departments rarely crossed state boundaries, where lines of authority were clear and people followed correct procedure.
>
> People didn't have any understanding of how to work across organizational lines, or with people at different levels. You were supposed to stay within your own unit, and when you had to go outside, the protocol was to talk to someone at your own level. I had to learn how to coordinate, delegate, and follow up in a hurry,

all in an atmosphere where everyone was wondering where the new power bases were. Traditionally, power came from direct control of resources. Plant had the capital funds and the construction program; Traffic had all the operators. Now in this new environment it's what you do with what you don't control that matters. You have to learn not to use your staff as a hammer, to ask questions of your opposite number yourself. All of that was new to us.

MacAllister recognized the problems involved in restructuring, but remained committed to matrix management. He saw the matrix as an opportunity to change from a militaristic style of management that demanded methods, procedures, practices, and structure, to a system that pushed decision-making responsibility down to where the information and action were. He encouraged contention over priorities at lower levels of the organization. With an orientation to service as "the customer sees it," the organization required increased interaction among the departments.

Under the traditional structure, the departments established their budgets independently of each other, without taking into account the effects on other departments. The budgets and the priorities they reflected rose all the way to the top before meeting any challenge. MacAllister's essential problem, then, was to redirect thinking to the demands of the external environment:

> How do you change the thought process of 31,000 people trained in a monopolistic environment to accept the challenges of competition? People were at various stages of anxiety. Many wanted to go back to the old situation and way of doing things. Remember, they've been trained to think in terms of methods, procedures, practices, and structures; in other words, to be administrators *par excellence*. Now we're asking them to think like entrepreneurs, to take risks, to be sensitive to the customer's preferences, to work with extended spans of supervision and control, to be flexible.

MacAllister took steps toward these ends with a new training program, but realized that he needed new methods to instill a competitive orientation in his employees. He brought together a "Willing the Future" management team and divided issues into three areas: (1) personnel management in the future; (2) the change to competitive, entrepreneurial thinking; (3) and the development of processes to encourage a proactive stance, "to spot issues as they emerged." More than 800 employees applied for the 120 available positions on the teams. MacAllister said:

> The excitement over the process of studying these issues permeated the organization; people kept asking about the results. Those on the committees were working nights and weekends on this. We changed the location of our annual management conference to maximize the number of people who could hear the task force presentations. The major effect was to signal to the organization that we were looking ahead, not to the past, and that in the future there would be lots of opportunity to participate and to contribute.

Service performance measures were abolished, as MacAllister emphasized the company's need to pay attention to sales volume. The Bell System maintained its extensive system of measures, which were still oriented to internal definitions of the role of service as performance. MacAllister decided that if Northwestern Bell was going to improve the quality of employees' work lives and orient employees to the external environment and customers' perceptions, it needed a new measurement system. TELSAM (for "telephone service attitude measurement") was developed to rate employee performance through random interviews with customers. TELSAM obliged employees to abandon traditional protocols for handling customers and to assess customer needs on an individual basis. Once TELSAM was adopted, office turnover dropped precipitously.

Rather than avoiding consumer councils as it had done in the past, Northwestern Bell actively sought them out to discuss concerns with interested groups. As telephone service was made more expensive by the elimination of cross-subsidies, the company argued that measured service would cost consumers less in the long run. In an effort to generate new markets, Northwestern Bell developed a targeted sales pitch on measured telephone service.

MacAllister was extremely concerned with broad issues of consumer awareness. In particular, it was imperative to retain AT&T's

traditional dedication to good service during the transition to a more competitive environment. It was important to help employees understand that doing a good job on basic service was a central part of the business, one that would not change. Becoming aggressive in advocating his own in-house marketing efforts, MacAllister appeared before the Telephone Pioneers—"a great, unrecognized service organization of retired employees"—and donated the services of a public relations manager to focus attention on the group's activities. He also developed a program of annual Spirit of Service awards to employees who exemplified the values of customer service. The award was a bronze statue of Angus McDonald, a legendary Bell System lineman who braved a severe storm to keep the lines open to a local hospital.

MacAllister himself looked forward to managing in the new environment. "For me," he said, "the need to meet the challenges of competition is like a new lease on life. I'm totally optimistic about the future, and I can sense a new enthusiasm and confidence in many of our people." As a realist, however, he also recognized that many employees still wanted "a magic wand to put things back, to fix all their problems. I suspect that some won't make it. They didn't sign on to work in a competitive environment. Many of them ought to leave for their own good. I think we'll see a lot of them taking early retirement or resigning."

Human Resource Issues

Throughout the BOCs, management was concerned about developing managers and employees who had right attitudes and skills for the new marketing approach. As one marketing manager put it:

> To appreciate the magnitude of changes that have taken place, it is necessary to understand the work environment in marketing prior to 1974. Even though the birth of the interconnect industry had taken place in 1968 with the Carterfone decision, competitive losses were few. We saw competitors as annoying upstarts who were interfering with our goal of providing good service to our customers.

In the Bell System, sales trainees had been former service representatives or installers; employee training emphasized product knowledge and "usage prospecting," which, in Bell language, referred to their nonaggressive sales approach. In the field, performance was judged by the same system used to evaluate management people in all departments. Incentives (promotions or monetary) did not exist; in fact, the corporation feared that incentive pay would lead to overselling to customers and would create a poor company image. Promotions were based on seniority and management's opinions of one's work, and top management jobs usually went to people from the technical departments. With the sales job selection process consisting of written math and verbal tests and role-playing exercises, the candidate's real hurdle was seen as "making it through the assessment process."

AT&T and Northwestern Bell enjoyed a relaxed work environment, where casually dressed employees viewed themselves as service consultants, not salespeople. As one insider said, "We were comfortable with our jobs, satisfied with our pay, and happy about the security of working for the telephone company." In 1980, however, an operating company manager talked about changes in marketing over the past seven years:

> In the business segment, maybe 25 percent to 30 percent of our people were ill equipped to deal with the highly competitive environment. Originally it was over half. It's been six years since we began to push the systems approach, and we're continuing to address the problem. Right now the business segment has about 4,600 people out of 30,000 for the company. Thirteen hundred are in the marketing function, 3,300 in services, which is mainly installation and repair. That is a very high labor intensity in services and too little in marketing. We're trying to reduce the size of our account executive territories. The average account executive is responsible for about $6 million in revenue; our goal is to get that down to $3 million to $4 million. The market is relatively elastic to sales effort.
>
> But we're limited by the labor costs in the service part of the organization. We need massive changes in customer premises equipment and service to take the service labor content out, and

we're on the brink of a series of changes that will mean substantially fewer people in service. The people who do that work are aware of that and very sensitive about it. Unfortunately, not many of them are cut out for the marketing side of the business.

The problem is that this requires different kinds of people than we were used to. We've begun to address the issues of recruitment and selection, and recruited people from college with business, computer, and finance degrees. Now we're offering competition, risk, speedier decisions, less security, more change.

Cultural and human resource problems were taking their toll on productivity. The company had tended to tolerate mediocrity, even in new hires. In the 1978 reorganization, salespeople who couldn't make it as account executives were reassigned to jobs at equivalent levels without demotion. But the costs of improperly placed human resources were running high, and there are few methods for incorporating cost control in human resource management.

A split between sales and service added to corporate difficulties. When a computerized market measurement system came on line, revenue results were measured for the first time, and the importance of revenue generation suddenly became clear. Although salespeople were not directly evaluated by these results, competitive wins and losses began to be followed by marketing staff, and a win/loss review process was initiated; if a sales representative lost an account, "explanation" interviews with the general manager soon followed.

In 1976 AT&T held its first national sales promotion, focusing on stimulating nationwide network usage. "Winning" was determined by the percentage increases in attained revenues. The corporation introduced competition among salespeople, a change that eroded much of the old comfort and job security. With winners getting the promotions in the years that followed, anxiety grew quickly within the sales departments.

New definitions of excellence and performance status permeated the organization. Perceptions developed that the top performers were in sales, and service employees reacted jealously as the personnel department hired more salespeople from outside instead of transferring them from inside service jobs. Although most didn't want to sell under the new conditions, their prestige and career opportunities were reduced, and they felt threatened in their unchanging roles.

Service people and some of the new sales representatives were also threatened by the new sales hires, and subsequently provided little assistance to them. New employees had the hardest time as an insufficiently developed sales training program and a lack of extensive telecommunications experience made it difficult for them to succeed. Personal antagonism and the lack of training accounted for much of the high attrition rate among the corporation's highly desired and desperately needed new trainees.

The new account executive position developed by McGill in the Bell Marketing System program did not bring the prestige and security that McGill envisioned; with separate vertical career paths and a lack of incentive compensations in the lower levels, one account executive noted that:

> They didn't have the right people for the job to begin with. I'm going to stay in marketing for most of my career. It's the key job in the Bell System, and the rewards are high. But there's a lot of anxiety and frustration in the job, and a lot of uncertainty and no real authority. The account executives are spread so thin that sometimes we're supposed to be responsible for so much that we can't possibly manage it well. Also, the career path falls outside the traditional system. People are level conscious and they want promotions.

To develop the professional career sales force and recognize individual achievement, the Bell System introduced an account executive certification program. To qualify for certification, a salesperson had to meet criteria in five areas: industry knowledge, account planning and management, team leadership, selling skills, and product knowledge. Although the program was originally intended to sell people on the account executive career path, insiders felt that most employees went into management because "they felt it was the only way to advance."

Although one high-level Northwestern Bell manager wanted to

recognize the professional expertise of account executives and give them the status and prestige that would keep them on the account executive career path, he viewed the bottom-line corporate issue as "a matter of turning a sow's ear into a silk purse." He acknowledged that some salespeople tried for certification and failed, but noted that the other jobs were found for them on the services side. "Since BMS and the certification program were introduced, 35 percent of the sales force was turned over. But the number who have actually been terminated under the certification program has been small—no more than 3 to 5 percent. The rest, he added, "found other jobs in the company or left voluntarily."

In the 1980s, over 50 percent of the account executives were certified. Managers, more comfortable with the evaluative process, coached their subordinates so they could meet the necessary criteria. The increased intercorporate communication helped diffuse the marketing approach. Additionally, since certification standards were high, a passing score immediately gave corporate recognition of an individual's abilities and potentials.

In September 1981 the Bell System's National Sales School opened in Denver. The three-month curriculum prepared account executives for the highly competitive environment. Selected sales instructors were former top account executives who were respected and know by their peers for sales results and professionalism. The workload for trainees was heavy, requiring evening and weekend commitments throughout the program's duration; tough standards and a 15 percent attrition rate meant that passing the assessment process only guaranteed admission.

Efforts to alter Bell's image began at the same time, as official corporate codes were adopted. Account executives were now to dress in coordinated suits, preferably dark blue or gray, in solids or pin stripes. Beards and mustaches were unacceptable. Cars driven by account executives were to seat at least four passengers comfortably and be less than six years old. The changes were strikingly parallel to other players' strategies within the information industry.

Reviewing the impact of BMS's changes on his department, one sales manager recalled:

> It was very tough at first. There were few support systems, and no reeducation process in place to help people adjust. There were

lots of meetings to explain the importance and necessity of change, but there was very little to help salespeople adapt the new corporate philosophy to practical application. We lost about 15 percent of our sales force when BMS was introduced, and according to our medical department, stress-related problems such as nervous exhaustion, chest pain, stomach ulcers, alcoholism, and drug abuse also increased.

On the other hand, there's no question that BMS, certification, the training school, and the other measures have been successful in achieving increased sales effectiveness and in transforming the marketing culture in the Bell System. Marketing departments are tougher, more competitive, more professional, and more powerful internally. Career opportunities in sales have opened up, and salespeople have doubled their earnings potential. The "survivors" in marketing seem to have adjusted to the new demands of their work environment and are comfortable with its higher risks and high rewards. You seldom find people in sales now who want predictability, safety, and security.

Some people feel that much of the anxiety might have been avoided with better preparation and more supportive management. Yet I wonder if we could have come so far so fast if we had waited until everyone was ready before we moved.

Staff Reductions

At most of the operating telephone companies, efforts to improve marketing and management capabilities were complicated by competitive needs to reduce the management work force. Although management reorganizations had solved parts of the marketing transition, the beefing up of management ranks outpaced the amounts of work that needed completion. A pyramid existed in traditional staffing practices; when a district-level manager was added, often whole supporting substructures came along. Each time an industry segment was developed and someone was appointed to manage it, the payroll grew disproportionately.

Northwestern Bell's approach toward consolidation had been to identify specific jobs that could be eliminated, rather than setting numerical quotas that department heads were expected to meet. AT&T, on the other hand, researched the managerial positions and used statistical analysis to determine where cutbacks would occur.

Thus, when state functions were consolidated into corporatewide network and business organizations, the task force found places to tighten the corporate belts, and broadened levels of control helped to decrease the number of management levels. Staffs were consolidated by critically evaluating and redefining job structures and reporting relationships.

The task force's report had recommended that Northwestern Bell eliminate 1,165 of its 8,500 management positions, including about 20 percent of third-, fourth-, and fifth-level positions (the three ranks just below the level of senior vice-president). Northwestern Bell planned accordingly, with about 870 of the recommended cuts were accepted immediately and another 100 cuts attributable to technical changes placed on hold. These were implemented when the associated engineering changes were completed.

AT&T developed an early retirement incentive plan and offered it to all upper-level managers as a way of spreading staff reductions; about 80 of the 500 executives accepted it. Since many of the managers were toward the end of their careers (their average age was fifty-six), high-level management at AT&T realized that only a handful would have left on their own. At Northwestern Bell, MacAllister commented:

> A number of people who originally said no to early retirement changed their minds after two or three months. They saw their friends leaving, and they knew what was ahead. But there are still those who should have retired and didn't perhaps because they felt comfortable in their current positions. We'll eventually have to confront the problem. People may be downgraded, displaced or asked to take assignments they don't want.

For middle-management cuts, Northwestern Bell relied mainly on attrition and strict hiring controls. Jean Smith, Northwestern Bell's director of personnel, discussed new relocation procedures within the company:

> We knew there would be about 500 jobs opening up due to attrition, so we set up centralized hiring controls to ensure that every

consideration was given to internal recruiting and transfer before going outside. We've stuck to our target of filling three out of four vacancies from inside; the only outside hires have been in sales and jobs requiring computer expertise. Prior to establishing critical review, only about 30 percent of our vacancies were filled from within.

As a result, the management work force was reduced from its peak of 8,600 employees in mid-1980 to 7,900 managers by the end of 1981, with the company pushing for 300 additional cuts by the end of 1982. Although the management downsizing effort was achieving its quantitative goals, Jean Smith cited some of its less tangible changes:

> Initially, the reaction to centralized control was negative. Every manager wants to make his own selection of people for job openings. But attitudes toward corporate personnel objectives have changed over the last year or so since the task force report. For many of our senior managers, it's now more fashionable to decrease the resources you use to get a job done than to increase them. I think it's a case of behavior influencing attitudes. If the direction of the behavior change is right, attitudes will change in time.

With reduced opportunities for promotions, people felt locked into current jobs and stuck in their careers, and Smith saw a dampening in morale as a growing company problem. The assistant vice-president handled issues directly; when asked about potential management positions, an employee recounted a past conversation: "If they're aspiring to management positions over the next year or two, they're going to be disappointed. On the other hand, he points out that by 1995 we'll turn over every middle-management position at least once." A specially arranged committee helped to facilitate lateral transfers. The changes were difficult to orchestrate, as the pre-BMS business, residence, and network structure called for a narrow kind of expertise that encouraged straight-line career paths in one segment. With the market-segmented organization, restrictions in movement were loosened somewhat, but marketing knowledge was required.

Problems extended beyond the functional and marketing areas. Where would the state CEOs and top managers come from? With downsizing in management satisfying requirements to reduce costs, it became harder to offer employees the breadth of experience they had enjoyed in the past. As careers matured, company insiders were cognizant of the top management succession problem.

AT&T combated specific training problems by instituting a four-week accelerated Advanced Management Program for high-potential management candidates. With an emphasis on finance, marketing, and "external factors," it oriented its training toward presidential and vice-presidential positions. Marketing required "creativity in problem solving," and Jack MacAllister spearheaded an Innovator's Council at Northwestern Bell. The group recognized creative company contributors and used company time to allow them to brainstorm and thrash out ideas. The council drew a socially diverse group of people from all levels of management, all segments, and all stages. As with the "Willing the Future" task force, the council was selected from a larger group of nominees from whom each council member solicited ideas and reported back. The underlying theme was clear: new criteria were prized as individuals were recognized for team performance and creativity, rather than using the traditional Bell practice of ranking individual performance against a static measure.

Interviewed in December 1980, MacAllister summarized his view of Northwestern Bell's future:

It's going to be a long evolutionary process, but I'm totally confident that we'll make it. I can sense a new enthusiasm in our people, a new willingness to handle the competitive challenges that face us in an entrepreneurial way. And that goes for the operating people as well as those in marketing.

Let me tell you a story. One of our people in business services figured out a way to cut over from Centrex to Dimension service without any loss of service. The telephone user didn't even know when the switch was thrown. It was also more efficient from the cost standpoint. Well, at one of our meetings, this person told about how he had done this at a recent installation. Another installer against the wall at the back of the room spoke up at the end and said, "Yeah, and he screwed us out of about thirty hours of overtime, too." The first installer came right back at him and said, "But we got a lot more work from this than there is in connecting a customer's own equipment." The room got very silent as people thought about it. You could almost see the reality of competition sinking home.

Part III
Crisis

In 1980 the FCC's momentous decision resulting from its Computer Inquiry II (CI-II) forced still more dramatic changes in AT&T's strategy and structure. The new ruling freed AT&T to compete in markets for customer premises equipment and enhanced telecommunications services. However, the company would be obliged to enter these markets through a free-standing subsidiary that was fully separated from Bell's regulated businesses.

Compliance with CI-II posed a series of thorny problems for AT&T and the operating companies. At AT&T, managers set about planning for the new subsidiary and designing ways to prevent cross-subsidies between regulated and nonregulated businesses. This work involved preparing a capitalization plan, setting up new administrative assignments, developing new engineering standards, reexamining personnel policies and labor agreements, and attending to a host of other details. At the same time, the company continued to press forward on programs to develop a marketing capability and to reorient employees for a competitive world. Once more, AT&T had to take a fresh, hard look at reducing its cost structure.

At Northwestern Bell, top managers faced similar problems. Although the Bell Marketing System had been implemented, much work remained to be done to develop and coordinate marketing efforts throughout the five-state region. Long traditions of state-level autonomy died hard. At the same time, Northwestern Bell anticipated continuing pressure on costs. To reduce head count, the company removed management layers and broadened spans of control. Company planners began contemplating further reorganization, this time around strategic business lines. Whether AT&T

Table III-1
The Bell System, 1980-1982

Industry environment:	Competition intensifies. Continued erosion of position in key markets. Rapid introduction of new technologies.
Policy environment:	Extreme uncertainty.
Regulatory justification:	Increasing concern with pricing and innovation as opposed to broader social objectives.
Regulatory challenge:	Piecemeal deregulation. Federal legislative solution unlikely. Antitrust case nearing conclusion.
Pressures for change:	Intensifying. New entrants, new technologies, public policy uncertainties.
Key management problems:	Paralysis of planning. Higher costs than competitors. Internal stress.
Internal environment and capacity for change:	Highly stressful. Problems with productivity, turf battles, and morale problems continuing. Increased job responsibilities and decentralized decision making at operating companies.

would permit Northwestern Bell to take such initiatives, however, remained an open question.

Still greater questions loomed over the efforts of AT&T and the operating companies to adapt to new circumstances. What direction would public policy take? Would CI-II stand up in the courts? Would a federal antitrust suit lead to additional restructuring? Would Congress, which had been considering comprehensive telecommunications legislation since the mid-1970s, finally act? How could AT&T predict the future? Could the future be influenced by lobbying or other corporate action?

The next two chapters describe how AT&T and Northwestern Bell endeavored to manage in a public policy environment of almost paralyzing uncertainty. Chapter 6 portrays AT&T's dilemma: How could it plan and prepare for a competitive environment when it had such little control over its future? In chapter 7, top managers at Northwestern Bell recount their plans and problems in managing during a period of intense pressure. Table III–1 charts the environment and challenges for the Bell System from 1980 to 1982, as discussed in chapters 6 and 7.

6
Coping with Regulatory Uncertainty

I n April 1980 the Federal Communications Commission rendered its final decision in its second Computer Inquiry (CI-II). Proclaimed FCC Chairman Charles D. Ferris: "Today we have removed the barricades from the door to the information age. Government will no longer be a barrier that prevents or delays the introduction of innovations in technology."

The Computer Inquiry II decision recognized that technological advances had eroded the distinction between data processing (computers) and data transmission (telephones)—a distinction the FCC had maintained for decades. CI-II created a new distinction between "basic services" (subject to regulation under the Communications Act of 1934) and "enhanced services" (which would be open to all competitors, including the Bell System). Basic services were those "limited to the common carrier offering of transmission capacity for the movement of information." In other words, "plain old telephone service" (POTS in Bell system language) was still considered a natural monopoly. Enhanced services, in contrast, combined "basic services with computer-processing applications that provided additional, different, or restructured information." CI-II also deregulated customer premises equipment, including telephones, PBXs, and computer terminals.

In CI-II the FCC acknowledged that the natural-monopoly model was no longer appropriate for the traditional telecommunications industry. While that realization had been acted on for some time by many electronic equipment suppliers, computer firms, and

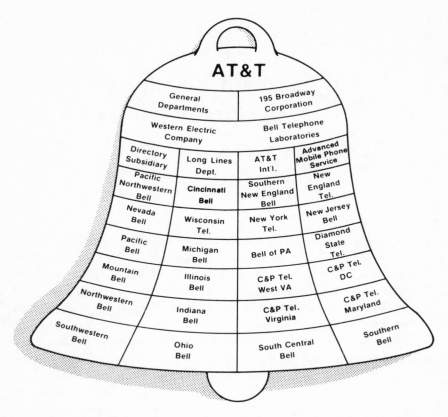

Source: George H. Bolling, *AT&T: Aftermath of Antitrust* (Washington, D.C.: National Defense University Press, 1983). Reproduction courtesy of National Defense University Press.

Figure 6–1. *AT&T Corporate Structure, 1982*

independent communications vendors, AT&T had been forbidden to join under the limitations of the 1956 consent decree and the FCC's earlier Computer Inquiry I (1966–1971).

As a result of CI-II, the Bell System was forced into another organizational change. It now had to create a new, separate subsidiary to manage the "nonregulated businesses" in enhanced services and customer premises equipment. This new subsidiary had to be separated from the parent at arm's length to preclude the possibility of cross-subsidies between regulated and nonregulated businesses.

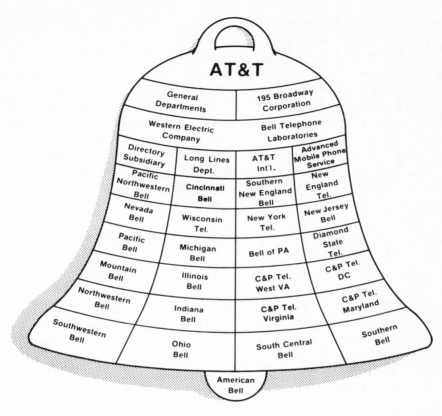

Source: George H. Bolling, *AT&T: Aftermath of Antitrust* (Washington, D.C.: National Defense University Press, 1983). Reproduction courtesy of National Defense University Press.

Figure 6–2. *Impacts of Computer Inquiry II on the AT&T Corporate Structure, 1983*

(See figures 6–1 and 6–2 for the organizational impacts of CI-II on AT&T).

Top executives at AT&T greeted CI-II with mixed feelings. On the one hand, they quickly recognized it as a landmark ("the most important FCC decision since 1934") and welcomed its general outline. The path was now open for the Bell system to compete vigorously in new markets. In this sense, the decision seemed to justify the strategic and structural shifts AT&T had made during the

1970s, when it reorganized to improve its competitive position and its marketing abilities.

On the other hand, CI-II raised as many questions as it answered. The decision provided little guidance for the restructuring of the Bell System. There were substantial ambiguities, for instance, about the administration of the arm's-length relationship required by the principle of "maximum separation." What safeguards would prevent cross-subsidies between the two sides of the business? How much administrative duplication would be necessary? How would Bell Labs and Western Electric be affected? What would happen to engineering standards in the System? Would the synergy between the research and production engineers and the marketing staff be lost?

CI-II also posed a number of more specific organizational problems. As John Segall, vice-president for corporate planning and financial management, pointed out:

> There had been little attempt by outsiders to evaluate the structural problems of the coming change. How do you capitalize the new company? How do you deal with the minority? What about the indenture agreements, the employee pension fund, relations with the union? The order wipes out all the efficiencies of unified organization throughout the System.

Looming over all these problems and questions was an even greater uncertainty. There was no guarantee that the FCC's order would stand up in court. CI-II directly contravened the 1956 consent decree by permitting AT&T to compete in data processing. Challenges could certainly come from would-be competitors worried that an unfettered AT&T might crush all competition in most markets. Some state public utility commissioners resented CI-II because it seemed a federal intrusion into state's rights. AT&T itself wanted to clarify or change specific language in the order that apparently limited the ability of the new subsidiary to compete effectively.

Pending public policies also threatened to render the order moot. In 1974 the Justice Department filed an antitrust suit against AT&T, alleging monopolization and conspiracy to monopolize the

U.S. market for telecommunications products and services. If successful, the suit would force AT&T to divest Western Electric and its ownership or partial interest in the twenty-three Bell operating companies. After six years in discovery, the case went to trial in a federal district court in Washington, D.C., early in 1981. AT&T's efforts to settle the case out of court had come to naught. Congress, meanwhile, seemed to be nearing passage of its most comprehensive legislation affecting telecommunications since 1934. Both houses were considering bills to deregulate the industry on terms broadly similar to the FCC's, although those bills differed in important respects.

For all of its own uncertainties, then, CI-II could be superseded on a number of fronts—in the courts, in the antitrust suit, or in Congress. The challenge confronting AT&T managers was to manage the ongoing transition of the Bell System from its historic position as a franchised monopoly to its new role as a competitive enterprise. That transition had to take place amid regulatory uncertainties, continuing internal corporate adaptation (from the previous ten years), and the ongoing need to keep the national communication network running.

Structural Change

Despite the public policy uncertainties, AT&T planned to comply with CI-II by March 1, 1982, and the process of reorganizing the post—CI-II company quickly proceeded. First, the company's highest governing body, the chairman's office, was redefined. Chairman Brown appointed Vice-Chairman James Olson to head those "departments within AT&T with prospectively unregulated responsibilities." Olson was also charged to design the structure of the new, fully separated subsidiary, which the press dubbed "Baby Bell." At the same time, William Ellinghaus was named to direct the traditional regulated telephone business. These two officers, along with Brown, Vice-Chairman and Chief Financial Officer William Cashel, Vice-President and General Counsel Howard Trienans, and Vice-President and Assistant to the Chairman Alvin von Auw, formed the office of the chairman.

AT&T followed this top-level realignment in subsequent

months with the reorganization of its headquarters' General Departments. Brown observed that:

> For a long time, senior management has been concerned about the mixed roles of the AT&T General Departments. On the one hand, the General Departments are responsible for such broad, corporate-level functions as finance, strategic planning, executive development, and government relations. On the other hand, they have many detailed operational responsibilities, such as design and operational methods for the Network and customer premises equipment. . . . Operational demands tend to divert executive officer attention from the overall corporate directional role. It is clear that the diverse business environment of the 1980s will require increasing attention to corporate-level strategies and plans. As the business becomes less monolithic and more diverse, appropriate relationships with increasingly independent disparate pieces will become vitally important in order to ensure a "sense of the whole."[1]

Brown then split corporate and operational functions, a task made easier by the fact that external market requirements and internal corporate objectives were not in conflict. Olson became responsible for business marketing and services and international operations; Ellinghaus's responsibilities included network planning and services, Long Lines, federal and state regulatory affairs, and nonbusiness marketing.

AT&T also coordinated and centralized corporate planning, financial management, public relations, public affairs, personnel, and labor relations under a new executive vice-president, Morris Tannenbaum, who reported directly to the chairman. During 1980 and 1981 managers were "seeded" throughout the general departments, helping to plan the transition in each function so that all personnel would know where to report once CI-II took effect. The final phases of the restructuring took place in 1981 and 1982, as plans for the BOCs, Bell Labs, Western Electric, and the new subsidiary were prepared.

Restructuring became the central theme of the semiannual meeting of operating company presidents in the fall of 1980. Chairman Brown and the AT&T staff made it clear that compliance with

CI-II would be standardized throughout the System. "The worst thing," said one staff executive, "would have been to have twenty different plans for compliance. This had to be coordinated at the national level." Centralization issues guided the corporation as BOC presidents studied restructuring issues and prepared guidelines that would match the larger corporate changes with their individualized needs. By the next presidents' meeting in the spring of 1981, Chairman Brown found general agreement that restructuring planning should be centralized and thus emanate from AT&T headquarters. At the end of that meeting, Brown directed AT&T's newly reorganized Corporate Planning Office to prepare Systemwide guidelines for the coming change by July 1.

Brooke Tunstall took responsibility for drafting these guidelines, and after an extremely intensive staff effort, the Corporate Planning Office produced three detailed volumes. They began by establishing the business's basic principles, including seventy fundamental assumptions about AT&T's strategy, technology, and organization. They also dealt with issues ranging from relationships between corporate staff and the regulated and competitive sectors, to "functions" like coin-operated phones or directory and information services.

The guidelines proposed a general structure for the Bell System. Earlier, Brown had written that "the contemplated structure" ought to transform "the current functionally oriented division of responsibilities at the highest levels to one of a small corporate staff and two profit centers, one operating in regulated, the other in unregulated markets."[2] Following this lead, the guidelines placed AT&T corporate headquarters at the top, presiding over both sectors. Under the national headquarters was Long Lines (minus its detariffed divisions, marketing and sales), the BOCs (less their detariffed functions), R&D, and manufacturing. The "detariffed/unregulated sector" included a third national headquarters, the new subsidiary (including the detariffed portions of Long Lines and the BOCs), AT&T International, and directory services.

The planning guidelines included information about BOC responsibilities that would be transferred to the deregulated subsidiary as well as specific recommendations for the restructuring of the BOCs. The market segment reorganization of 1978–1979 would

serve as the basis for the changes. Most of the old business segment—about 80 percent of the account executives and customer
service representatives and between 40 and 60 percent of their administrative support, according to one manager—would move over
to the new subsidiary. The remaining staff in business marketing
would combine with most of the old residence segment into a new
BOC marketing department. The network segment and the other
traditional corporate functions would be only slightly affected by
the reorganization.

As for the new subsidiary, the guidelines offered only bare details. The subsidiary would consist of two divisions, each spanning
six geographical regions across the United States. A business systems division would be organized according to the principles of the
Bell Marketing System (BMS), and a consumer products division
would be responsible for customer premises equipment.

In the fall of 1981, AT&T's planning officers anxiously sought
the opinions of managers elsewhere in the System on the reorganization guidelines. According to the company's timetable, the BOCs
were supposed to respond with comments and proposed budgets by
the fall of 1981. It was hoped that the new subsidiary would be
capitalized and that transition teams would be set up to staff it by
the end of the year. Early in 1982, those personnel in the BOCs
who would follow their work to the new subsidiary were to begin
reporting on a dotted-line basis to the regional officers of Baby Bell.

A New Marketing Spirit

The restructuring capped a decade of organizational turmoil inside
the Bell system. AT&T had already moved from its traditional functional structure toward the market segment organization. Technological, competitive, and regulatory pressures had driven earlier reorganizations, so the Bell system was reasonably well prepared for
the next major upheaval. Yet in a company as large as AT&T—an
organization of about a million people—much remained to be accomplished from previous structural changes. In the fall of 1981,
for instance, two BOCs had not yet completed the 1978 reorganization. Many more BOCs were still grappling with the problems of

adapting to a competitive marketplace with personnel inherited from the more serene era of the franchised monopoly.

During the 1970s, corporate staff had focused on developing the new marketing spirit and the organization to go along with it. With market segmentation and new professionals in key staff and sales positions, senior executives' objectives were mostly achieved. Reviewing the changes, Robert Casale, assistant vice-president and national director of business sales, felt that

> BMS was the cornerstone of our sales organization. It enabled us to evaluate and investigate how our operating companies were doing relative to each other. The establishment of consistent guidelines, the creation of the segments, and the straight-lining of reporting were very helpful. We could then structure the recruitment, education, training, and performance appraisal of the new sales force. BMS and the programs designed to support it achieved a great deal.

But problems remained with the new system's implementation. One sales manager pointed out:

> We had a field organization with no confidence in itself. The staff told the line what to do. We were suffering from a literal interpretation of the new guidelines. It was just like the Green Book [the traditional performance measurement manual] in the old days. The staff thought people on the line were idiots. People on the line thought the staff had lost touch with reality. The external environment was changing radically, and the results in 1979 and 1980 were terribly uneven.

In the fall of 1981, however, Casale believed things were looking up. He remarked:

> The incentive compensation package is well designed. The career path in sales is now formulated, and the steps to advancement are well articulated. Account executive candidates must submit a portfolio that demonstrates knowledge of the client industry, our products, and the techniques of systems selling as well as the ability to prepare a good account plan. Beyond these, candidates must obviously have good selling skills.

The certification process is threatening, even traumatic, for some of our older sales force. A lot of these feelings depend on how well the process is managed. To some extent, the certification board makes a qualitative judgment on a candidate's abilities, but at least the standards are consistent. Candidates have one year to qualify for certification. Something like only 10 percent will pass on the first try, but by the end of the year, about 70 or 75 percent of the candidates will make it. During that year, we can look at the reasons why a candidate didn't make it and work on helping him or her out. There are development programs of differing lengths for people with differing abilities.

In 1981, AT&T opened a National Sales Training School in Denver. All account executives and assistants would be required to pass through a fifteen-day program in selling techniques. In addition, account executives and assistants were given some training in organization development and business strategy. Most of their training, however, occurred on the job. "Sales training is very disciplined," said one manager. "I think we're making substantial progress," Casale added. "We can now achieve the objectives of BMS. There is enough recognition now. Most of the old resistance is gone. It will work."

On October 1, 1981, the senior national sales managers at AT&T assumed control of sales throughout the BOCs on a dotted-line basis. They were also at work on improving management systems to support the BMS. New appraisal standards would tie sales performance to strategic objectives under the guidance of sales quota review boards.

A New Management Style

Although the greatest changes at AT&T occurred in marketing, there were substantial adjustments in human resources throughout the System. Every employee had to come to terms with the company's new strategy and environment. Robert Beck, assistant vice-president for human resources staffing and development, portrayed this period as one of "quiet revolution." According to Beck, the Bell System's central challenge in 1981 was still to develop managers who could cope with the increasing uncertainties of the business. The traditional qualities that AT&T had sought in its managers— intellectual abilities, administrative and interpersonal skills, and motivation to succeed—remained relevant, but the company was now obliged to look for other qualities as well: entrepreneurial skills and the ability to take risks and to manage under uncertain conditions. In short, the Bell System learned to cultivate a new management style.

Under the traditional workings of the Bell system, managers often spent their career inside one function. Only at the level of operations vice-president (the number two officer in the BOCs) were the functions pulled together. The new structures of the 1970s and 1980s pushed decision making down several levels in the organization and required many more skilled managers with both old and new qualities. Throughout the 1970s, human resources managers at AT&T looked for ways to recruit and train managers with both a high tolerance for ambiguity and skill in dealing with it.

Robert Beck's staff spent years assembling a data base from which to work. Since World War II, AT&T had maintained a network of management assessment centers. By the 1970s the company had amassed an immense amount of historical raw data on System employees. This information, along with data culled from employment records, was gradually computerized and provided Beck and his staff with profiles of some 285,000 Bell System managers, as well as many more nonmanagement employees. (Employees of Western Electric and Bell Labs were not included in the data base.)

While this work was underway, said Beck, "We began a study of human resources strategies for the 1980s. We knew that the future would require a different sort of manager, more entrepreneurial and risk taking." Researching other companies across a whole range of industries, AT&T learned how managers were developed who could successfully cope with unpredictability and risk.

New human resources strategies included tougher employment standards and screening. Beck explained:

> The general employment offices which principally hired nonmanagement personnel required major changes. We had to cut out all

kinds of bad practices and simply get the best qualified candidates. As for management employees, we look for people with the potential to become top-flight executives, and we've tightened college recruitment standards. Lots of jobs are fairly routine from day to day. Others, like planning assignments, organization development jobs, and high-level staff work, immediately demand this ability. We're more circumspect about putting people in these positions.

For higher-level needs, an Executive Continuity Program was initiated to replace the old career track for executive managers. Highly talented people were provided opportunities to climb to top management positions, developing skills as they met the challenges of difficult management tasks early in their careers. Other high-level development programs included carefully structured job assignments that offered senior managers needed marketing training, which complemented their technical and functional experience. Post rotations (experience in at least two BOCs and at AT&T headquarters) became mandatory, and Bell's Advanced Management Program operated for middle-level managers.

Cutbacks and New Rewards

The new pressures on AT&T headquarters required human resources managers to deal with other thorny issues: some long-time Bell managers were simply unable to function as effectively in the new competitive environment. Additionally, the demands of the marketplace required a slimmer, more cost-efficient organization. The choice was either to let these managers go or to switch them to positions where they could be productive. Along with the problems of restructuring, then, came the need for "resizing."

The company's assessment programs helped distinguish the managers of the future from those who would be encouraged to pursue new careers outside the Bell system. Beck felt that the program worked fairly well on a voluntary basis, and it was expanded to address various kinds of surplus situations.

Attrition, however, even when speeded by outplacement, did not keep pace with the need to shrink the System's managerial ranks. In the first three quarters of 1981, AT&T hired about 60,000 people for a net increase of some 8,000 employees; few vacancies occurred in the operations that needed to reduce personnel. So with streamlining and resizing came the idea of altering traditional spans of control. In the BOCs, which had five layers of management strongly entrenched below the officers, AT&T human resources managers wanted to eliminate at least one level where possible to create a more flexible structure. Beck argued for this change:

> Increasing spans of control improved jobs by increasing responsibility, and it saved money. More importantly, it allowed us to tailor the organization according to the demands of the environment. It permitted us to organize jobs around new functions rather than around traditional functions. In short, we can organize to meet our business strategy rather than a hundred-year-old form.

Resizing encountered strong support in the Bell System, but also strong opposition. Shrinking the organization meant increased outplacement, delayed promotions, and changed reward systems for the remaining personnel. According to one manager: "Every BOC has committees and subcommittees studying the resizing issue, weighing the pros and cons, and there's a lot of resistance. It's going to be a while before this gets fully implemented."

The means of persuasion included redefining jobs and titles, and offering incentives to encourage more teamwork. As Beck put it:

> There are other kinds of rewards than money. You can use informal means as well as formal. Greater spans of control and skip-level reporting represent new challenges, which can be motivators. You can also change titles. Upgrading titles need not be eyewash or a sham; it is recognizing that times and jobs have changed. The other thing you can do is modify reward systems to reflect the new style of management. We are developing a compensation program geared to promoting more teamwork. We hope to minimize consciousness of levels and status in this way.

The Uncertainties of Telecommunications Policy

With plans for splitting the business formulated and some organizational reforms under way, Bell System officers were anxious to move ahead. "The major problem for top management is not so much strategy anymore," said Brooke Tunstall. "That is largely decided. We have to get the regulatory issues settled and get freedom in the marketplace." However, AT&T's ability to respond to the demands of CI-II—and, more important, to competitive challenges—was inhibited by continuing uncertainties about the decision and about public policies being generated in other forums.

The major issues in national telecommunications policy could be sorted out according to the stakeholders most affected, although, of course, many of these issues were interdependent. From the public's point of view, the value of inexpensive, universal telephone service—the original justification for AT&T's franchised monopoly—remained constant. Few parties disagreed that the United States offered the best telephone service in the world, or that a single telephone network under one management was important for national security. But, ran a counterargument, the public interest was also served by competition, since competition ensured that companies would emphasize efficiency and innovation and would strive to keep costs and prices down. Moreover, there was no shortage of critics who argued that Bell's monopoly bred inefficiencies and stifled innovation.

Competition also served the needs of another set of stakeholders—the rapidly growing numbers of companies already offering products and services in communications, data processing, and office systems. Such companies included not only traditional participants like GTE and other independent telephone companies, but also computer and high-tech businesses and many other large companies like IBM, ITT, Exxon, Sears, Aetna Life and Casualty, and United Technologies, all of which were diversifying out of previously distinct markets. These potential competitors were concerned with such issues as the terms of access to the Bell network and the exact rules under which AT&T would be permitted to compete in customer premises equipment and enhanced services.

A third set of stakeholders were the three million shareholders and one million employees of the Bell System itself. Indeed, consideration of the rights and interests of these groups was the principal reason that some regulators and legislators were unwilling to force AT&T to divest its business in competitive markets like customer premises equipment and data transmission. AT&T's management, moreover, was concerned that any settlement protect the interests of these groups.

The competing jurisdictions of federal and state policymakers made formulating an equitable policy increasingly complicated. At the end of 1981, state and federal regulatory agencies, Congress, and the federal courts were each vying for primacy in settling the future of the telecommunications industry. Besides the CI-II decision, the FCC was active in a variety of other ways affecting the Bell System and competition in the industry. For example, in 1981 the FCC allocated 50 percent of available frequencies to AT&T for its Advanced Mobile Phone Service, a new technology that would provide portable cellular telephone service for people on the move. Some analysts believed that cellular mobile phone service would eventually supersede the traditional central offices of the local exchange business. Still pending before the FCC was an inquiry into the Uniform System of Accounts, which could force a major change in the way AT&T reported its financial information to regulators.

In addition to the FCC, several other federal agencies were following developments in the telecommunications industry with particular interest. The most important of these were the National Telecommunications and Information Agency in the Department of Commerce (which arbitrated international communications policy) and the Department of Defense. Several agencies not specifically charged with communications issues, including the Equal Employment Opportunity Commission (EEOC) and the General Accounting Office (GAO), also had considerable impact on the Bell System.

State regulation of telecommunications presented another range of problems to the Bell System. AT&T provided services in more than fifty separate jurisdictions. Every new product or rate adjustment was subject to hearings in each one. The BOCs were normally responsible for filings before these bodies, although corporate staff at AT&T monitored rate hearings and coordinated systemwide policies. AT&T and the BOCs also tracked the proceedings of forty-eight of the fifty state legislatures. In any given year, more than a thousand bills might have implications for the Bell System. Many of these were trivial, but some—such as those dealing with measured services, taxes, coin phone rates, and directory services—affected BOC revenues substantially.

Federal and state courts also frequently heard cases vital to the

Bell System's interests. In 1981 the importance of judicial decisions was vividly driven home to Bell's managers in two important cases. In the criminal antitrust suit, AT&T faced the possibility of divestiture of Western Electric and its ownership of the BOCs. Top managers were clearly worried about the potential outcomes of the suit. They had tried and failed to settle the case out of court on two occasions—negotiations that AT&T's lawyers had dubbed "Quagmires I and II." In July 1981, after the prosecution rested its case, AT&T's lawyers had petitioned for a dismissal. Two months later, however, the presiding judge, Harold H. Greene, had refused. He commented that "the testimony and the documentary evidence adduced by the Government demonstrate that the Bell System had violated the antitrust laws in a number of ways. On the three principal factual issues, the evidence sustains the Government's basic contentions, and the burden is on the defendants to refute the factual showings."[3]

Even if this suit was settled or appealed in AT&T's favor, there remained scores of private antitrust suits filed against AT&T over the years. Some of these could have competitive implications, even though they did not affect the structure of the Bell system. In 1981, for instance, a federal court awarded MCI (a competitor in long-distance transmission) triple damages of $1.8 billion from AT&T— the largest such settlement in history. While this decision was under appeal, MCI was preparing to file a second suit against Bell for $3 billion.

CI-II and Its Critics

The FCC's final decision in CI-II came under siege from the moment of its announcement. Most of the controversy revolved around how AT&T would allocate resources in the future under the arm's-length relationship. Rivals and would-be competitors worried that AT&T could apply the tremendous profits of its regulated businesses or the impressive abilities of Bell Labs to help Baby Bell dominate its new markets. Antitrust lawyers and economists echoed the same points. The separate subsidiary, testified one, was "a half-solution" and "a policy snare or delusion." The GAO endorsed this view in a widely quoted report published in the fall of 1981:

> By a single conglomerate subsidiary . . . the Commission, we feel, is setting the stage for the creation of a huge deregulated entity that would be endowed from the moment of its creation with substantial market dominance, as well as a significant potential for internal cross-subsidy and a host of other anticompetitive actions. By the same token, by refraining from imposing structural separation in such vitally important areas as manufacturing and applied research and development, the Commission left a considerable potential for cross-subsidy and improper sharing of inside information and has rendered its own regulatory tasks . . . immeasurably more difficult.[4]

CI-II was also challenged on more specific legal grounds. In addition to petitions for reconsideration filed before the FCC itself, the order was challenged in the courts. Several parties, including some state public utility commissions and the U.S. Department of Justice, were contesting the FCC's right to preempt local jurisdictions or to overturn the 1956 consent decree.

State Public Utility Commissions

State public utility commissions (PUCs) protested CI-II on several grounds, including states' rights. Some simply announced that they would refuse to recognize CI-II. Others resisted the FCC's power to make changes affecting the process of separating interstate from intrastate costs. From this perspective, CI-II asserted federal jurisdiction over customer premises equipment formerly regulated by the states. "Clearly, the state commissioners don't like CI-II," said Al Partoll, vice-president for state regulatory matters at AT&T headquarters.

> And I understand their rationale. Under the new order, the cost of local service is going to up a lot, doubling in the next ten years. The long-distance business has been subsidizing local service for most of this century. If long-distance revenues cannot subsidize residential customers, the old capital recovery system has to be abandoned. This directly implicates the state regulatory process and puts pressure on state regulators.

AT&T's Objections

During 1980 and 1981, AT&T registered its own complaints about CI-II. Bell managers agreed with the utility commissioners that detariffing customer premises equipment would wreak havoc with traditional methods of allocating costs and revenues (separations and settlements), and that this would tend to magnify the disparity between interstate and intrastate tolls. In particular, they were not certain how they could unbundle the costs of customer premises equipment from interstate transmission costs, since the same equipment was used for both local and long-distance service. According to Partoll, however, "All accounting for terminal equipment had to be off the books of the operating companies by the time the order takes effect. That represents about $6 billion in revenues shifted to other parts of the [Bell] System."

A second problem was the inability of the fully separated subsidiary to own and operate transmission facilities. The worry here, according to Arch McGill, was that "the separate subsidiary would be constrained from being as able as its domestic and foreign competitors to respond rapidly to unique customer-integrated systems requirements and to provide customized solutions."[5] There was some concern, for instance, that, under some interpretations of CI-II, AT&T might not be allowed to offer a distributed data service it had already announced. An FCC Order of Reconsideration modified CI-II to permit the Bell subsidiary to build transmission links between multiple customer buildings in a single location, such as an industrial park. However, many Bell managers were dissatisfied with this solution because it failed to outline a clear general policy.

AT&T also petitioned the FCC for reconsideration on the basis that it has not adequately addressed such threshold matters as rules for depreciation, capital recovery, and asset valuation. The company felt that these matters had to be resolved before the new subsidiary could begin to offer detariffed customer premises equipment. At stake, according to the company, was the quality of service to millions of customers, as well as hundreds of millions of dollars. To forbid the immediate transfer of assets would create confusion among customers and might also increase their dissatisfaction when they understood the administrative waste involved. AT&T hoped, then, that the FCC would permit the subsidiary to administer all regulated customer premises equipment and, further, that personnel from the new subsidiary and the operating companies would be allowed to work together for a period after the compliance date to ease the transfer of customers and of assets.

In October 1981 the FCC refused AT&T's request. The commission asserted that the book value of the assets was not a reflection of their economic value, and that their economic value was impossible to determine; therefore, it limited the capitalization of the separate subsidiary to new equipment only. It also ruled that the operating companies could maintain equipment for the business customers of the separate subsidiary for eighteen months thereafter. In recognition of the difficult issues remaining to be resolved, however, the FCC also extended the compliance date for separation to January 1, 1983.

A Legislative Settlement?

The many legal and political challenges to CI-II—including some of AT&T's own—led AT&T's top managers to advocate a legislative settlement of national telecommunications policy in the early 1980s. Their hope was to replace the uneven docket-by-docket advance of deregulation with a more definitive constitutional statement. As Chairman Brown put it in Senate testimony:

> The charter which governs the communications industry was written in 1934. . . . A regulatory charter based on the experience of the first third of this century is not adequate to cope with the environment of the 1980s and 1990s. We—the American public and American business—need a contemporary, comprehensive declaration by Congress of the nation's telecommunications policy.[6]

Between 1976 (when AT&T first proposed new legislation) and 1981, Congress considered eleven major communications bills. The general thrust of all of these was similar: toward the deregulation of the industry. There were, however, substantial differences among them on such issues as comprehensiveness, the scope of competition, and provisions to restructure the Bell System, as well as on more technical points. Apart from a general interest in deregulation, congressional attention to telecommunications was spurred by several factors: strenuous lobbying by interested parties, interbranch rivalry with the Justice Department and the FCC, and a need to lend some finality to federal policy. On October 7—the same day that the FCC turned down AT&T's petition for the immediate transfer of assets—the Senate approved the Telecommunications Competition and Deregulation Act (S. 898) by a vote of 90 to 4.

The Senate bill differed from CI-II in a number of important respects. In the first place, S. 898 was more comprehensive; it covered several issues not addressed in the FCC order, including accounting and depreciation rules, access charges, and interconnection bottlenecks. It would permit the deregulated subsidiary (which it called a "fully separated affiliate") to operate its own transmission facilities. As for the initial capitalization of the new subsidiary, S. 898 authorized the FCC to appoint a joint committee from its own ranks and from state utility commissions to determine the fair and proper valuation of assets.

The Senate bill also spelled out the details of the arm's-length relationship between AT&T and its deregulated subsidiary. S. 898 specified that the new entity could

> have no more than one director in common, no common officers or employees, and must maintain separate books and records. [It] cannot own property jointly with its parent or regulated affiliates and must carry out its own marketing, sales, maintenance, operations, advertising, installation, production, and R&D.

Although senior Bell managers disagreed with some of its features, they embraced S. 898 as "a bill we can live with." They were unhappy with the requirement that AT&T allow its rivals to connect into the basic telephone network on the same terms as AT&T Long Lines, without allowance for Bell's prior research and development costs. S. 898 also put significant restrictions on both the regulated and the unregulated businesses. The regulated companies, for instance, would be required to purchase from 8 percent to 20 percent of certain categories of supplies from outside vendors. The unregulated subsidiary would be prohibited from benefiting from any research partially funded by the regulated companies unless those results were also provided free of charge to competitors.

AT&T would also be prohibited from entering the cable television business and other markets such as alarm services. At the same time, AT&T was required to set up another separate subsidiary for traditional time and weather services. In the words of Chairman Brown, S. 898 might have been "the most significant milestone yet in the effort to forge legislation that will establish new national policy," although, he added, it was "tough, double tough, on the Bell System because in mandating competition in the marketplace, it puts the reins on us, but gives spurs to everyone else."[7]

One reason that AT&T preferred a legislative settlement—even one that put on the reins—was procedural and political. It was easier to lobby the Congress than the FCC. "The commission is not as open as Congress," said Daniel Culkin, an assistant vice-president for federal regulatory matters, who added:

> We have to deal with them in formal pleadings so that other parties can comment or appeal. The whole relationship is defined by an adversarial legal setting. Our filings have to be worded very carefully and in a public way. When you're dealing with the FCC, moreover, you're never through. CI-II is a good example. The decision left out a lot of issues which have to be settled in separate filings. There are more things to discuss and more uncertainty about what this business actually is. CI-II is silent about whether the subsidiary can be vertically integrated. Does that mean that it can or that it can't? The decision doesn't give us much in the way of guidelines for forming the subsidiary or in valuing its assets. The FCC also wanted to look at R&D provisions, the cross-subsidy issue, and license contracts separately. All this takes time and affects our ability to offer products and services in the marketplace. The commissioners are not incompetent nor do they lack dedication to their work. It's just that the process is necessarily slow.

With Congress, on the other hand, AT&T enjoyed a less formal and adversarial relationship. According to Scott Shepherd, a director of public affairs:

We have constant interaction with congressional staffers. But they often come to us. Staffers have to draw on our resources and expertise to get good information. A legislative aide to Senator Howard Baker told us that elected officials spend something like 70 to 80 percent of their time dealing with constituents' problems. They have little time to give to shepherding complex issues through a long legislative process. As a result, they have to rely on credible lobbyists for research.

Although Bell managers regarded congressional action as superior to the FCC ruling, the legislative process had its own frustrations. Foremost among these were the long lead times between the introduction of a bill and its enactment, and the numbers of problematic amendments that could crop up along the way. S. 898 had passed the Senate but was not yet final, and AT&T did not know what modifications the House would propose.

In 1980 the House subcommittee on telecommunications, then chaired by Congressman Lionel Van Deerlin (D–California) had approved a communications deregulation bill that differed from S. 898 in small ways. However, the full House had not voted on this bill. In 1981 the new chairman, Congressman Timothy Wirth (D–Colorado) was critical of both S. 898 and CI-II. As he put it, "What we want to do is to deregulate only when the forces of competition are ready to govern the industry." He argued that a "structural manipulation" of the Bell System would not be sufficient to guarantee effective competition in the industry, and that it wasn't clear that consumers would benefit from such an approach without very strict safeguards. Wirth was also interested in broadening the scope of the legislation to cover the whole communications industry, including cable and broadcast issues. From AT&T's point of view, such expansion of the bill would effectively end hopes for a quick resolution of national telecommunications policy, because it would involve much wider debate and lobbying from many more interested parties. On December 10, Wirth filed the Telecommunications Act of 1981 (H. R. 5158). The bill, he said, "encourages the development of competition while offering specific protection against cross-subsidy of unregulated services or equipment by regulated activities."[8]

At the end of 1981, Chairman Brown summed up AT&T's political uncertainties:

> We stand midway through the largest government antitrust suit in history. We are in the midst of congressional consideration of yet another set of legislative proposals for restructuring our industry. And we are reorganizing our business on a scale and at a pace unmatched in history in response to a regulatory order that may or may not prevail.

Continuing on this theme, Brown said:

> We are caught on the horns of a dilemma that, were it not so serious, would be ludicrous. On the one hand, some people say that not until the antitrust case has been decided should the Congress enact telecommunications legislation. That could be years hence. On the other hand, the administration says that not until the enactment of legislation will it withdraw the antitrust suit. I submit that it is intolerable that an urgently needed national decision should be paralyzed over an Alphonse and Gaston argument over who should go first. It is time . . . for somebody to act.[9]

Despite the indeterminate future, AT&T plunged ahead with its compliance with CI-II. On November 30, AT&T's capitalization plans were filed for its new subsidiary's first product, a distributed data service. Senior managers were disappointed that the FCC had extended the date for restructuring to January 1, 1983, but remained optimistic that Congress would enact an acceptable version of a deregulation bill and that the federal antitrust case could be settled out of court during 1982. "It might be quite a while before things settle out after that," observed Alvin von Auw. But, he added, "there is still one constituency yet to be heard from—the public. Once the public feels the impact of deregulation, there may be policy adjustments down the road."

In von Auw's view, the most important issue facing the Bell System in the coming years would be "the graceful management of repricing"—educating the public as to the full meaning of a decade of fundamental change in the telecommunications industry. AT&T's

public relations department was preparing a massive program to explain "the biggest restructuring of any business in corporate history" to customers, shareholders, and employees.

The recasting of the Bell System from a franchised monopoly to a competitive company "has been and will be an inelegant process, one fraught with complications," said another top executive. Yet for many senior managers the most important point was to preserve the values of quality and service bequeathed to the Bell System by Theodore Vail. Commented von Auw:

> There has been a lot of talk recently about resource allocation decisions and about managing both the regulated and competitive sides of the business strictly by the bottom line. As long as we remember that we are still a service company accountable to the public, we'll be all right. But if the day ever comes that we run this business by the numbers alone, then that will be the day to begin talking about the decline and fall of the Bell System.

7

Managing Change at Northwestern Bell: Part II

In December 1980, roughly eighteen months after the implementation of the market segment organization at Northwestern Bell and nine months after the FCC's CI-II decision, Jack MacAllister announced further changes in Northwestern Bell's organizational structure. First, he combined the residence and network vice-president positions into one, and then he transferred responsibility for central support services (primarily real property, maintenance, and motor vehicles) between high-level managers. The changes went counter to the 1978 reorganization guidelines, in which the one fixed rule was a separate corporate officer for each segment.

MacAllister then straight-lined the residence segment. Residence managers in the five states were to report directly to Dick McCormick, senior vice-president–residence/network, rather than to their respective state CEOs. Except for business segment marketing and services, McCormick was to have line authority over all operations.

State CEOs were left without any direct operations responsibility. Under the new organization, they reported directly to the new senior vice-president–finance and external affairs, and together they had primary responsibility for rate regulation, legislative affairs, public relations, and consumer relations. Their second major responsibility was to provide financial and service assurance in support of their regulatory and external affairs role. As MacAllister explained, "regulation, quality of service, and profitability are inseparable in this business."

Matrix Management

The financial and service assurance functions of the state CEOs were exercised through matrix teams in each state (which the state CEOS continued to chair). These teams were the primary mechanism for coordinating expense budgets, revenue targets, and income commitments. They also solved service-related problems that cut across market segments within a particular state. Taking care not to lose direct contact with each market, MacAllister then appointed each state CEO to a corporate-level committee. The Minnesota CEO became the first state CEO to sit on the Executive Council, and another became part of the Corporate Budget Committee.

With the need to combine competitive needs in marketing with regulated and deregulated services under CI-II, McCormick felt that:

> From what I heard there wasn't a lot of enthusiasm on the part of AT&T for this new structure. They saw it as a deviation from the 1978 guidelines. I thought it would be very unpopular with the state CEOs. Even though they don't report to me, there will still have to be a strong dotted-line relationship between them and the operating people. MacAllister has asked them to be the final word on the bottom line, and they'll still need to know what's going on in operations in order to assure good service. But if this structure will help on the regulatory side of the business, I'm all for it. We have a monumental job ahead of us there. I just didn't see that they were hampered by too heavy an operating burden.

Howard Doerr, senior vice-president—finance and external affairs, sensed that all the administrative benefits of the market segment structure would not be accomplished until the residence segment was straight-lined. Under the current structure, if an issue involved residence, managers had to go to five state CEOs, and action was taken only after the five direct contacts had been made. Questions quickly arose concerning the state CEOs' objectivity on budget matters. At times the duality of the state CEO's position created conflicts. Often it was wise to get the network and business segments to absorb more than their share of cuts, whereas at other times it looked as though the state CEO was sacrificing his own units to avoid seeming biased, and his position ended up appearing suspect.

The primary reason for the organizational change was to get effective representation with regulatory, legislative, and political constituencies. Under the new organization, state CEOs lost no time worrying about day-to-day operations and service, but devoted their attention exclusively to their primary function: dealing with the external environment. The state CEO job had been an operating position, but the changes redefined the role as that of a marketer, selling the need for good service (and hence good earnings) to regulators and politicians. As an orchestrator of all aspects of the regulatory process, the state CEO worked externally with constituencies and internally with the matrix teams, batting out internal operating service or cost issues. With Northwestern Bell needing about $500 million to $600 million in rate relief between 1980 and 1985, it was the state CEO's job to accomplish this feat.

Northwestern Bell set about implementing the matrix organization in 1980. The realignment of the senior vice-president's responsibilities provided the opportunity to expand the state CEO's job, and the organization moved completely away from dependence on line operating authority to the broader responsibilities of profit center management. MacAllister realized that the shift was traumatic for the state CEOs, who had grown up with the idea that line authority equaled power and influence. During the 1978 reorganization planning, it had become apparent that it would be too much to take away all their direct authority before they had the opportunity to learn how to manage without it.

The transition time eliminated duplicate functions in management. A structure consistently segmented by market enhanced ability to coordinate resource allocation priorities across state boundaries. The new state CEO role created an advocate for the customer and public inside the company—"an advocate," said MacAllister, "who was independent of the operating people responsible for providing service, free to articulate the customer's point of view, and well positioned to get action with his influence on rates, earnings commitments, and expense budgets." Northwestern Bell now had high-level managers who devoted their energies to the BOC's cases before the state regulators, legislatures, and other outside constituencies.

Strategic Planning

At the same time MacAllister was realigning the senior vice-presidents' responsibilities and straight-lining the chief operating officers, he also created a new strategic planning unit. Strategic planning proposals developed by the unit were reviewed monthly by teams of line operating and marketing managers, tested by the Executive Council, and then presented to a new board-level strategic planning committee. This group, said MacAllister, consisted of "myself and some of our more entrepreneurial outside directors." He explained that

> If we're going to get anywhere with strategic planning, I have to make the planning process highly visible. Board involvement will help accomplish that. This will be the "first" time the board of directors is involved in the long-range planning process. We'll also have monthly reports to top management, and both televised and written presentations to middle managers. We need to sell people on the need to get involved in strategic issues. Strategic planning isn't just a top-management exercise, it's a way of thinking about business decisions at all levels.

Traditionally, the operating company had given very little attention to pricing, market structure, or the actions of other telecommunications vendors. With poor linkage between the five individual state plans and Northwestern Bell's corporate plan, the planning system lacked a sense of corporate mission. The director of the new strategic planning unit, Larry Kappel, spent the summer of 1980 visiting other companies, talking to people at AT&T, getting input from consultants, and reading the academic literature on strategic planning. He noted:

> The most obvious difference between our system and the one used by other businesses is that we did not plan by discrete business units. Many telephone people didn't believe you could allocate

network costs to various market segments, for example. So, the first issue was, could we identify strategic business units in the Bell system?

Cross-subsidies presented problems for the operating companies. Competitors accused the BOC of using them to protect the regulated monopoly, yet CI-II's delineations remained unclear on the issue. Strategic planning systems that resulted in the movement of resources from one strategic business unit to another could be viewed as a cross-subsidy system, but cash flows taken from one unit were often used to "subsidize" the growth of another. In a partly regulated, partly competitive environment, would it be possible to allocate capital toward high-potential strategic business units and away from those with low profitability and growth prospects? Management felt that the close relationship between strategic planning, capital resource allocation, and financial planning prevented the BOC from basing the lines of business solely on market distinctions such as business versus residence, because that approach shed no light on capital spending issues. Common competitors or common delivery systems cut across industry segments and had significant impacts on the return on investment (ROI).

Trapped in this dilemma, the BOC's high-level managers met with strategic planning executives at AT&T. For Northwestern Bell, the meeting's main purpose was to achieve an accurate definition from AT&T about what constituted a business unit for strategic planning. MacAllister and his colleagues discussed Northwestern Bell's work with AT&T, and explained that the operating company intended to use some kind of strategic business units as the basis for long-range planning. As a safeguard for the parent corporation, they displayed alternative approaches.

MacAllister then volunteered the BOC as the operating company trial horse for developing a Bell system strategic planning approach.

Lines of Business

The lines of business further separated the market segments that McGill had introduced seven years before, thereby forcing the business to respond in a more competitive fashion. As an example, the distinction between intraexchange and interexchange service was based both on traditional operating and regulatory considerations, and on the different competitive characteristics and ROIs of local loop versus long-distance telecommunications. The distinction between terminal products and business terminal products reflected differences in user characteristics (residence and small-business customers versus large corporations), and the delivery systems used to supply customers (retail stores stocked with standard products versus custom-designed systems sold through account executives).

The identification of coin and charge-a-call service as a separate business could be attributed to financial and regulatory considerations; it was hoped that breaking out the full costs of this service would help the company obtain higher rates from public utility commissions. The information service category was intended to legitimize AT&T's entry into new electronic information services, extending its traditional Yellow Pages and directory assistance operations. Newspapers and other publishing trade groups, however, were quick to fight this competitive extension; they lobbied the government to restrain AT&T to its traditional business as a provider of voice services.

Strategic Business Units

The strategic planning unit began by assembling data for a portfolio analysis of Northwestern Bell's lines of business, including market size, share, growth rates, and predicted profitability. For the first time, the company broke down profits other than by states—a difficult task, as formal cost methods were nonexistent. Methodologies became clearer when AT&T examined a cost study prepared for regulatory purposes and reconstituted it by lines of business to provide a historic base for sales, costs, profits, and growth. Grids were prepared for each year from 1980 to 1985 to show how the BOC's overall portfolio would evolve.

Problems developed as local telephone service showed low profitability and a slowly growing market, whereas the electronic services market had high profit potential. Could the operating company handle an opposite product strategy? Should it? The director of strategic planning commented on the changes in the business's approach:

> The chairman of General Mills faced a similar problem with the flour-milling business. Traditionally, it was the core of their business, but it wasn't where the money was made. So they divested it. But to apply the same logic to the Bell system boggles people's minds. It boggles my mind. Bell people have always regarded local service as the core of the business.
>
> Most people here, in fact, don't think of local service as a separate business at all. The operations people have always treated the network as a single system, and our current organizational structure has reinforced this by setting up the network segment as a basic building block.

For strategic purposes, however, the network segment divided into two businesses: intraexchange (local service) and interexchange (long-distance service), with striking competitive implications due to regulatory rules and market growth potentials. While operating people maintained the system-wide network, responsibilities for the intraexchange and interexchange equipment were split in the network organization. Northwestern Bell started treating the operation as separate businesses, implicitly assuming that long-distance service made no financial contributions to local service; it was as if local service got the same access charge contributions from all providers of interexchange service. With the Justice Department suit pending, the change was tenuous, as there were hints that distinctions between local and interexchange services were increasingly subject to public scrutiny.

Capital spending plans used the most immediate application of the strategic analysis. With regulation, projects that looked good in terms of their ROI were pursued on a stand-alone basis as it was recognized that costs were covered completely through regulation's rate recovery process. In the competitive environment, capital projects had to be evaluated both on their own merits and for their impact on the business's strategic needs. Opportunity costs dictated spending decisions and discretionary spending became crucial, as

Northwestern Bell now lacked the regulatory approval to "justify" rate increases easily to questioning customers.

Larry Kappel pondered the changes imposed by the strategic perspective:

> I think the decision on FACS (a project to automate the assignment of cable parts, which also reduced labor operating costs) will be a real barometer on how far we have come in learning how to think strategically. The FACS project can be justified by traditional ROI calculations as a stand-alone project, and it is being pushed very hard by the network people at AT&T. But the strategic requirements for the exchange business are, first, to increase prices through better management of the regulatory process and, second, to hold down costs, especially capital costs. Essentially, we need to improve the revenue productivity of capital. By this criterion, if the main benefit of a project is to save expense dollars, which is what FACS does, then you shouldn't do it.

Strategic plans and mission concepts were developed for each line of business once a basic portfolio analysis was completed. Six strategy teams (corresponding to each line of business) composed of technical managers and led by corresponding marketing or revenue-producing department managers formulated individualized strategies for each line of business. They set objectives, oversaw the preparation of strategic plans, communicated the plans to the Executive Council, and oversaw their implementation. Team members were senior enough to command resources, but not officer-level executives like the senior vice-presidents or state CEOs. Northwestern Bell's thinking was that fifth-level or lower people would be more familiar with the operating implications of strategy and more likely to analyze their lines of business in detail.

There was a kink in the process, however. The lines of business and the strategy teams did not directly correspond to the current organizational format. The teams quite possibly represented the first time the organization first developed a strategy and *then* the appropriate organization. Once again, movements and job redefinitions were required.

But the influence of strategy on organization showed clearly in the planning for the deregulated subsidiary. Learning quickly how to maneuver its market segments (a Consumer Products Division and a Business Systems Division), the organization shifted and followed the product-line distinctions used in establishing the separate lines of business for single terminals (sold through Phone-Center stores) and complex customer premises equipment (used by business).

MacAllister saw significant results following the first year's strategic planning approach. He expanded on the management implications wrought by the changes:

> A focus on strategic business units such as our lines of business forces interaction and attention to corporate goals. The direction the government is going will require every line of business to float on its own bottom. We've set up the strategic planning process to involve as many managers as possible, especially at the middle levels where it is easy to lose sight of our overall situation. The overlay of strategy teams provides another basis for communication and participation across departmental boundary lines, since no line of business has impact on just one function or segment. This is particularly important in a matrix organization such as ours, which demands participation and involvement in each other's decisions. If too much emphasis is placed on segment or functional goods, the matrix falls apart.

MacAllister was wise to emphasize employees' positive actions throughout the changes:

> To make the transition from traditional to strategic thinking, I pay close attention to the kinds of questions I ask and how I ask them. Instead of asking what's wrong with service or why, I try to ask people what they are doing to improve service. In budget overruns, I try not to ask why they overrun their budgets; I ask them what they can still do to meet their bottom-line commitments.

Reviewing the changing environment with which the company was coping and the kind of management it now required, he continued:

I also try to stimulate thought in the area of risk management. I ask people what they would do if they owned the business, and I try to get across that the corporation isn't going to come down on them with all its might if they drop the ball. It is ironic. People who had been here longer told me, "Don't rock the boat, don't make waves." Now they're all working for me. The real paradox in the Bell System is that the people who make it to the top have a total disregard for playing it safe. All the officers at Northwestern Bell were known as mavericks at one time in their careers.

For many, however, risk taking and strategic thinking represented a fundamental change in their thinking. In the past, the hallmark of a good engineering manager had been his ability to hit his construction budget on the nose, regardless of what might have happened elsewhere in the business. MacAllister noted that in 1980

We had a $48 million underrun in revenues. One way we made up the lost cash flow was by spending only $570 million of our $610 million capital budget. Together with savings from management downsizing and other cost-cutting measures, we were able to overachieve our commitment on the bottom line. This took significant management intervention; in the past we'd either get back the lost revenues in rate increases or miss our objective. The kind of short-term responsiveness we achieved this year doesn't mean we are thinking strategically yet. But at least people are demonstrating an awareness that performance in one area affects activities elsewhere in the corporation. That's a step in the right direction.

Consolidation and Disaggregation

While developing the strategic planning approach, Northwestern Bell also planned for restructuring according to CI-II. AT&T's voluminous guidelines had reached the BOCs in June 1981. As in the 1978 market segment reorganization, the guidelines proposed general templates for the new structure but allowed individual operating companies to propose specific plans and negotiate variations to suit their particular circumstances. The operating companies were to respond with financial plans, personnel forecasts, and organization charts by September 1, 1981.

The AT&T guidelines called for a two-phase transition. The first phase, *consolidation,* was to be implemented on October 1, 1982. Under consolidation, the management structure of the deregulated subsidiary was established down to the regional level; managers of operating company functions ultimately destined for the subsidiary would report to the new hierarchy on a dotted-line basis. Direct operating, financial, and personnel authority would remain within the operating companies. The consolidated or dual mode of operation was intended to provide a transition period for planning the full separation of the regulated and deregulated sectors of the Bell System.

The second phase, *disaggregation,* completed the separation of the regulated entity and the nonregulated sectors. Disaggregation required the movement of personnel and activities to separate locations; the transfer of capital assets, expenses, and revenue streams; and the assumption of line operating authority by "deregulated" managers for all detariffed or unregulated services. In a few cases, activities would continue to be performed jointly during the disaggregation phase until the necessary deregulated subsidiary's administrative support mechanisms could be created.

Although the original FCC order called for implementation of the disaggregation by March 1, 1982, AT&T petitioned the FCC for more time to plan a smooth transition. As the authors of the Northwestern Bell restructuring plan put it:

> Complete disaggregation on March 1, 1982, while technically feasible, would cause serious short-term inefficiencies. We can anticipate costly relocations of employees, revamping of buildings, new leases, employee surpluses, and a number of other unresolved transition problems.

During this period, the FCC was concerned that immediate transfer of all customer premises equipment to the new subsidiary would provide it with undue financial and market power, since it would then have a much larger installed base than its competitors. AT&T protested that the "bifurcation" approach would confuse

customers about who was responsible for billing and service.
Howard Doerr participated in transition planning and commented
on the service aspects of a regulated/competitive transition:

> Bifurcation would actually minimize the impact of disaggregation
> on the operating companies. If we don't transfer the assets, reve-
> nues, or equipment, then we don't transfer very many people.
> We've leased an empty department store across the street from our
> headquarters building and moved in all the business segment's
> sales, service, and staff people to get ready for disaggregation. Un-
> der bifurcation we may have to reevaluate that.
>
> But the impact on us is minor compared to the horrendous
> problems it would create for our customers, especially the ones
> with large, complex systems and frequent changes in equipment.
> Suppose someone who already has a PBX buys an add-on from
> the subsidiary. Who does he call for service if he doesn't know
> where the problem is? How does he straighten out billing prob-
> lems? The state public utility commissions are upset about bifur-
> cation, too. They expect to see some pressure on rates when you
> take out subsidies from terminals and enhanced service, as you
> have to do if it's to be competitive. Bifurcation leaves most of the
> underdepreciated value in terminal equipment in the regulated en-
> tity, where it will continue as part of the rate base. With the "flash
> cut" we're seeking, more of that would be taken out and rates for
> basic service could be that much lower.

Although it was unclear whether AT&T would succeed in re-
versing the FCC's bifurcation approach, planning proceeded with
positive assumptions; upon disaggregation, the new separate subsidiary would be responsible for all customer premises equipment.

Transition According to CI-II

Shortly after Northwestern Bell received the guidelines, MacAllister
asked Dick McCormick to serve as the company's transition officer
to manage the implementation of CI-II's requirements. He also appointed a transition council, with eight officers chairing a transition
team composed of fourth- and fifth-level managers who were responsible for studying one aspect of the restructuring. MacAllister

did not participate directly in planning for the new organization as he had in 1978. He preferred to involve himself in the development of strategic planning and other long-range concerns.

As Northwestern Bell's restructuring plan took shape, in the words of one report, "it became apparent that a number of issues might have to be resolved in ways different from those suggested by AT&T guidelines." A number of undetermined issues concerned the development of the regulated sector's marketing capabilities, which was the task that Northwestern Bell considered the most crucial. Consequently, their approach to the new functional alignments varied from the systemwide plan in two respects.

First, the company moved faster than AT&T planners envisioned. The guidelines recommended that no major restructuring actions should be taken immediately, and that during consolidation, the operating companies were expected to continue using the 1978 market structure based on business, residence, and network segments. The primary structural change during the consolidation was the establishment of dotted-line relationships with the new subsidiary managers. The planners at Northwestern Bell, however, said:

> We believe we should begin to operate with an organization structure labeled "consolidation phase" no later than January 1, 1982. We believe this will be necessary if we are to maintain strong financial accountability and workable tracking mechanisms, and if we are to take full advantage of the dotted-line reporting relationships with AT&T during the transition.
>
> Our reorganization experience of 1978 and 1980 suggested that we must begin to restructure now if we are to implement the plan on January 1. Therefore, we propose to have our top-level appointments completed by September 15. All department, division, and district assignments would be made by October 1, 1981.

In effect, Northwestern Bell moved immediately to a structure similar to one AT&T had proposed for the 1985 time frame. This future structure had been included to give the operating companies a sense of the longer-term directions that should be incorporated in near-term planning.

A second variation involved the placement of the regulated marketing organization. Under Northwestern Bell's plan, the vice-president–marketing would report to the senior vice-president and chief operating officer, whose new job included responsibility for both network and marketing. He would not report to MacAllister, as the AT&T guideline recommended. MacAllister explained:

> I wanted the marketing organization to report through the senior vice-president/chief operating office to involve him, to get closer coordination between marketing and network operations, and to give me more time for strategic planning, emerging issues, management succession planning, and the management development of our capacity for change. The AT&T plan was based on the idea that the regulated marketing organization should have direct access to the president. But there's no reason I can't work with the vice-president–marketing on market development issues under the structure we've proposed. I'm trying to get the idea established that it's acceptable for managers to go to the person responsible, to get at the source of a problem or need, regardless of what level he's at. This has been difficult for the people at AT&T to understand.

Northwestern Bell also identified other key marketing issues that it proposed to resolve jointly with AT&T. It recommended that, whereas detailed pricing work and preparation of rate case testimony should remain with the regulatory functions, regulated marketing should have a strong voice in setting price levels. At Northwestern Bell, marketing would set target prices for various services and would have final approval authority over rates before they were filed in regulatory proceedings. The company also pointed out that detailed pricing design for network services was very similar throughout the Bell System and that it would make sense to perform this function on a regional or national level.

Northwestern Bell then questioned AT&T guidelines that called for dividing the existing business segment into large-business and general-business modules and keeping these separate from the residence segment. The operating company challenged AT&T's recommmendation that separate general-business and residence service centers ought to be established. Northwestern Bell argued that small-business and residential customers were similar in market characteristics, service needs, and selling approaches, particularly in the rural areas that made up much of the company's territory. In Northwestern Bell's view, joint marketing strategies and combined service centers for general-business and residence customers should be acceptable under the new structure.

Northwestern Bell also questioned AT&T's directions for splitting the large-business and general-business modules. Each of the modules was supposed to have its own face-to-face, on-premises sales force of communications service executives (CSEs). Under AT&T resource guidelines, 97 CSEs would be responsible for 1,334 large-business accounts at Northwestern Bell, and 25 CSEs in the general-business module would be responsible for 14,356 accounts that were too small to be included in the large-business segment but were nevertheless eligible for account management. Northwestern Bell felt that the overall effectiveness of its sales resources could be increased by concentrating all CSEs in the large-business segment under one manager, and that AT&T guidelines provided fewer CSEs than would be necessary given the volume of work and the responsiveness of revenues to sales effort. In contrast to the account management approach for large businesses, Northwestern Bell wanted to rely on mass marketing techniques and customer-initiated sales through the Business Service Centers, with referral to large-business CSEs for face-to-face selling when required by special circumstances.

With CSE resources focused on large-business accounts, Northwestern Bell felt that CSEs should be positioned with higher-level decision makers in the customer's organization, as was the current practice with account executives, instead of with lower-level telecommunications managers as the guidelines recommended. The operating company, however, was concerned that until a highly professional sales force of CSEs could be developed to replace the account executives being transferred to the new subsidiary, large-business customers might think "that the Bell System's problem solvers all went with the deregulated subsidiary, and that the deregulated entity was only a regulated commodity-service utility." Northwestern Bell believed it was "imperative to convince its customers and other constituencies that the future of network services was exciting, challenging, and on the leading edge of technology."

The company proposed that each operating company find several individuals with advanced degrees in electrical engineering or similar disciplines and excellent oral and written communications skills. These people would serve as resident technologists—as academic, intellectual futurists. They would keep abreast of the state of the art in telecommunications and would position the regulated operating company as the service vendor that could always bring the most advanced technology to solve the customer's business telecommunications problems. They would support the sales force in highly technical systems design work and would make their services available to specific customer groups, trade associations, and the general media within Northwestern Bell's territory.

In addition to marketing issues, Northwestern Bell's transition teams identified several other concerns. As the first step in its restructuring, the company disaggregated the residence organization effective August 1, 1981. The disaggregation was similar to the dispersion of residence functions in the guidelines. The new position of vice-president–distribution services integrated all installation, testing, and maintenance activities from the central office to the customer's terminal, thereby eliminating the split in responsibility between network and residence services for installation, testing, and maintenance that had existed since the 1978 market segment reorganization. Northwestern Bell also pointed out that the restructuring had a significant impact on regulatory proceedings. The AT&T guidelines assumed that the trend toward increased subsidies from interstate to local service would be reversed upon disaggregation, that settlement with independent telephone companies would be reduced, and that a variety of regulated charges to the deregulated subsidiary would be acceptable to the FCC as proposed by AT&T. These assumptions tended to raise income and ROI forecasts for the regulated sector, and reduced pressure for rate increases on regulated service. Northwestern Bell questioned whether these assumptions were realistic. In addition, the company pointed out:

> Classical regulatory theory argues for lower return on equity in businesses that exhibit less risk. We must develop the rationale that conveys the requirements for continued improvement in earnings for the regulated industry, which remains a highly competitive and risky business.

Some employees within Northwestern Bell saw a gradual diminution in reliance on the state teams for decision making. Although there was extensive communication between state CEOs and line managers on regulatory and public affairs issues, reliance on the formal matrix of state teams had declined. One manager attributed this to a shift in the state CEO responsibility away from budgeting. He said:

> So much of our expense at the state level represents corporate allocations that it's hard to budget from the bottom up. With 40 to 50 percent of expenses representing pensions, overhead, depreciation, and the like, we've found it necessary to do more budget development from the top down. If there's a problem, the state CEOs would look for further savings within their respective states. But recently, with the success we've been having on rate cases, there hasn't been too much need for that.

Ted Meridith, the state CEO for Minnesota, agreed that with better financial performance in his state, his reliance on the matrix had diminished somewhat. He commented on the new communication flows and management's role in that change:

> In the early stages of change in my job, the matrix had tremendous value in teaching us to communicate. Now that we've gone through the transition, I'm not sure whether it will continue to be necessary or not. Some of the things we originally did through the matrix teams now get done through informal communications and peer relations. One thing that won't change—the state CEO absolutely has to know what's going on in every function within his state in order to handle his regulatory and external affairs work. The matrix structure provides a basis for staying in close touch. It's important that Jack MacAllister has always given us the support we need.

Northwestern Bell in the Future

MacAllister remained committed to the matrix organization structure and was pleased to see its value recognized in the AT&T guidelines. However, he still continued to reiterate his support for the principles of matrix management. He commented on management's role in the volatile business:

> We had kind of a showdown during our last management confer-
> ence. The state CEOs felt that they weren't being apprised of
> things going on in the company they needed to know. I told them
> that their job was to know anything in the company they needed
> to know. They're big boys, and they're being paid big money. I
> said, if you not invited to a meeting you need to attend, invite
> yourself. I asked them if I had ever failed to back them up, or if
> they didn't have full authority to do their jobs. Later, two CEOs
> came to me privately and said, yes, we think we need a little kick
> in the butt.
>
>   The matrix only provides the format. People have to do the
> participating and communicating. Most of the criticism of the ma-
> trix, that "no one's really responsible," is a throwback to the old
> macho idea that you can hold individual managers accountable
> for different parts of the business. You can't. It's too complex. And
> Computer Inquiry II doesn't change that.

During late 1981, MacAllister was spending much of his time thinking about Northwestern Bell's future. Interviewed on January 7, 1982, he said:

> My most important objective is to develop our capacity to change.
> If there's one thing we've learned over the past few years, it's that
> change and uncertainty are inescapable in this business. We need
> to make strategic planning an integral part of our management
> thought processes. We need to learn how to keep close tabs on
> trends outside the company and to spot emerging issues. Perhaps
> the most important thing is to maintain our confidence in the fu-
> ture and in our own abilities. Sometimes we tend to lose sight of
> how strong a position we're in. Here I sit running a company that
> represents only 4 percent of the Bell System, yet we have over $5
> billion in assets and $500 million in net income. With that kind
> of base, plus the ability to handle changes we've demonstrated
> over the last five years, I don't think there's anything any legisla-
> tive, regulatory, or judicial body can do to us that will leave us
> stranded, without opportunity or hope for the future.

Part IV
Aftermath

In January 1982, AT&T agreed to divest its twenty-two operating companies, including Northwestern Bell. In exchange, the corporation received open entry into both national and international markets, with only its long-distance voice communication services continuing under regulation. Some $80 billion in assets and roughly 750,000 employees were affected by the divestiture, which took effect on January 1, 1984. The Modification of Final Judgment (MFJ) was the federal judiciary's response to the ambiguities and uncertainties of CI-II.

At U S WEST (the regional holding company that would then own Northwestern Bell), top managers greeted the MFJ enthusiastically as they set about shaping their responses to technological, competitive, and regulatory trends. While U S WEST was now in a position similar to that of the old Bell System, Jack MacAllister continued to press for further industry deregulation. Refusing to remain idle while the industry continued to change, U S WEST set itself up as a financial holding company. Three of its subsidiaries handled telephone communication services.

At AT&T, employees were unsure of the demands of the new environment. Chairman Brown felt that the divestiture agreement "confirmed the central elements of what we believe to be national policy and disposes of debilitating uncertainties." AT&T retained its name and continued the work of gearing up for competitive challenges; restructuring helped the new AT&T to form its deregulated divisions and shift thousands of employees into new positions.

AT&T had prepared for competition for years; indeed, it seemed amply prepared for still more change. Yet, despite its preparation, the company experienced difficulties in its new environment as revenues plummeted.

As head of U S WEST, MacAllister responded to the MFJ by fighting regulatory constraints while seeking new opportunities for growth. Top executives emphasized the positive aspects of the industry changes and created new programs that focused on cost consciousness.

After the divestiture, both AT&T and U S WEST faced regulated and deregulated markets. Both organizations faced dramatic internal corporate change. U S WEST successfully altered its image and directions; in 1985 AT&T was still floundering. Was AT&T, with its ingrained complexity of procedures, too far removed from the marketplace? Could a pyramid leadership structure motivate employees sufficiently? Low company morale plagued both organizations, yet U S WEST faced the crisis with bold action, whereas AT&T restructured, rewarding employees with marketing skills and implementing new incentive programs. Were the two strategies so different?

With a progressive management style, U S WEST sought direct market contact, guided by internally developed long-term strategic planning. AT&T attempted to motivate former monopolists while looking for areas where costs could be cut. How did divestiture affect those areas? How could workers' skills be adapted to both corporations' new needs? Could the remaining work be organized so that employees could train across numerous fields? What were the costs of such a process?

Strategic planning decisions and employees' adaptations to new roles demanded top management's attention, but in the deregulated environment, risk and uncertainty faced both organizations. What factors led to U S WEST's success? What hampered AT&T's efforts to penetrate new markets? As both corporations clung to Vail's belief in the "quality of service," the marketplace awaited them, ready to reveal the successes and the failures of their corporate adaptations. Table IV–1 charts the environment and challenges facing AT&T and U S WEST from 1982 to 1985.

Table IV–1
AT&T and U S WEST, 1982–1985

Industry environment:	Fierce competition in long-distance and customer premises equipment markets. Accelerating pace of technological change.
Policy environment:	Becoming clear. Continuing regulation, principally of local exchange.
Regulatory justification:	Local exchange still regarded as natural monopoly.
Regulatory challenge:	Antitrust settlement resolves many issues, but continuing pressure on natural-monopoly argument persists.
Pressures for change:	Continuing from predictable sources. Competitors in redefined industries.
Key management problems:	At AT&T: Define new strategy. Organize to enter new business. Lower costs and rebuild morale. At U S WEST: Create new identity. Define strategy and policy options. Set up organizational structure and systems. Lower costs.
Internal environment and capacity for change:	At AT&T: Highly stressful. Continuing morale, productivity, and turnover problems. Difficulties developing competitive skills. Rapidly shrinking organization. At U S WEST: Optimistic management at top levels. More anxiety lower down. Programs to manage ongoing change in place. Decentralized decision making. Slowly shrinking organization.

8
The Breakdown of Traditional Regulation

During most of the twentieth century, the telecommunications industry was characterized by few opportunities for technological change. The regulatory process, which largely confined itself to setting rates, remained fairly constant from year to year. Regulation also supported an elaborate system of cross-subsidies to benefit residential customers in the name of providing universal telephone service. Under this traditional form of regulation, AT&T did not have to contend with shortened product cycles, changing products, or a changing industry environment.

Over time, therefore, telecommunications regulation tended to slow down or eliminate benefits arising from major technological innovations.[1] AT&T's large capital expenditures and complex accounting for depreciation tended to mask inefficient operations. In the absence of open market competition, AT&T's operating costs seemed necessary and appropriate, and were thus "naturally" included in rate-setting decisions. The Bell System lacked incentives to develop or adopt new technological methods or cost-efficient production processes. Charges were passed along to consumers who could not choose alternative products. Because of the complexity and interdependence of the telephone business and the conventional nature of traditional regulatory thinking, then, public policy makers had difficulty comprehending or controlling the underlying operations or cost structure of the Bell System.

In the 1970s and early 1980s, new technologies acted as catalysts to help break down traditional regulatory assumptions. Digital transmission allowed the simultaneous passage of both voice and data signals. Powerful data-processing companies supplied a steady stream of increasingly sophisticated equipment that redefined the methods and content of information exchanges and created new market segments. Microwave relay stations and satellites offered low-cost alternatives to the entrenched telephone network. These new technologies altered the industry's cost structure and placed great pressure not only on the Bell system, but also on its regulators. As an AT&T insider pointed out, "Technological change did not determine the future of the industry; it was one of the sponsors of that future."[2]

The FCC's ruling in Computer Inquiry II attempted to regulate these technological developments in an effort to preserve the traditional regulatory regime. If communications were narrowly defined as sending and receiving information, but not processing it, then communications would remain a natural monopoly, and the public interest could best be served. Thus CI-II aimed to clarify the distinction between communications and data processing and to protect the former under regulation.

Yet beyond the relationship between AT&T and the FCC, new entrants continued to offer new products and services and helped accelerate the process of obliterating traditional regulatory distinctions. After 1980, CI-II's inadequacies became all too apparent. Technological innovations—new switching equipment and customer premises equipment—were not being adopted in an economically efficient manner, especially by AT&T. Indeed, CI-II's strict guidelines for structural separation of regulated and nonregulated businesses impeded AT&T's efforts to offer its own new services and equipment. Arm's-length separation of organizational units made it impossible for AT&T to realize benefits of administrative coordination in developing innovations. Because the economic value of new services depended on integration with the network, and because CI-II blocked such integration, the Bell System and ultimately the public suffered.

One possible public policy response to this problem would have been to grant AT&T exclusive ability to offer new products and services in telecommunications. This would mean that other technical restrictions such as interconnection conditions (standards), product choices, and pricing schemes would also be regulated. By the early 1980s, however, such a policy approach seemed remote from reality. With competition from new entrants intensifying, the policy would have involved a significant reversal of prevailing trends and an increase in the public bureaucracy at considerable public expense. Moreover, such a policy would have given the Bell System—a private corporation, after all—market control extending far beyond a natural monopolist's copper-wire voice communications network.

Throughout the 1970s, despite its protests, the Bell System actually used regulation as a competitive weapon. For example, AT&T often used the regulatory system to its advantage as delays and formal hearings helped stall decisions that might assist new competitors. Indeed, it has been noted that one of regulation's primary effects has been to slow down the rate of change in an industry. If technological developments do not occur and an industry structure remains constant, there is little incentive to allow new forms of competition or to tamper with the regulated player's status. Such a situation clearly benefits the player who might otherwise have lost markets to new competitors. Potential entrants, then, are made worse off, because they cannot gain pieces of the market that they perceive as newly developing or changing.[3] AT&T took advantage of such barriers to entry to buy time once it became apparent that public agencies were inclined to promote competition. These barriers were particularly effective against smaller, start-up ventures that lacked extensive resources to fight expensive legal battles.

Even if successful in legal battling, entrants into telecommunications faced additional problems created by regulation. When allowed into the regulated market, they were generally required to compensate the regulated company for its losses or to prove to the regulators that their entry would not have a significant impact on existing players.[4] Such difficult, costly processes helped to secure the regulated player's position.

Despite many rounds of stalling, market forces had become strong enough by the late 1970s that the Bell System's regulated position was being questioned in fundamental ways. AT&T had anticipated these movements and had begun to shift from its traditional role as a manufacturer toward a new role as a sales and marketing organization. In this way, AT&T responded to piecemeal deregulation and the erosion of specific markets by new entrants. These actions, moreover, helped the company learn new methods of operating in the competitive environment.

The Policy Dilemma

When working with technological change and an evolving industry, it is difficult to create policies that can answer to an industry's needs, both immediately and for the future. Because technological change is evolutionary in nature, it becomes important for regulators to create a policy solution that appropriately matches the evolutionary nature of the change. Unfortunately, public policies often respond to industry conditions at a particular point in time. CI-II posed tremendous difficulty to many industry players because it was a static solution imposed on a dynamic technology and industry.

The ability to alter operations and implement longer-term strategic plans was vitally important to AT&T. CI-II constrained product development and limited sales at the point in time when the corporation was gearing up to compete. Throughout the 1970s and early 1980s, AT&T had worked to lower costs and prepare for price competition. That task, along with developing marketing skills, were its primary challenges. Through the arm's-length subsidiary separations rule, however, CI-II hindered the corporation as it attempted to control costs, develop new technologies, and fully adapt competitively. The policy, either intentionally or inadvertently, disrupted both operations and planning.

Looking at the regulatory process as part of a competitive strategy, a player can employ a range of tactics to secure its market position.[5] In the case of AT&T, regulation helped the corporation block new entry. Although regulation did limit the overall rate of return, it was less strong in controlling both the management of the company and individual service pricing. Regulation could not force AT&T to introduce new products or technologies, but it could discourage efficient production and distribution. Such problems tended to surface when regulators later unraveled historical rate-making equations and subsequently had difficulty determining the economic value of new technologies or determining cost patterns of cross-subsidies.

In AT&T's case, competitive battles were fought primarily through public forums (courts, Congress, regulatory commissions). The public bore these costs through taxation and a skewed rate structure. The Bell System's adaptation to competition occurred within the bounds of the regulatory rate-making processes, and its costs could again be passed along to the consumer. As its own supplier under regulation, AT&T controlled its own costs, but incentives of the system encouraged unusual priorities. Management tended to be more concerned with high-quality service than with the appropriateness of a product to consumers' needs.

Cutting the Gordian Knot

By the early 1980s, the illogic and the cost of traditional telecommunications regulation were becoming unbearable. Indeed, regulation seemed to serve no one's interests. Competitors and would-be entrants protested the Bell System's potential to cross-subsidize. AT&T itself was unhappy with CI-II's restrictions and concerned about the progress of the criminal antitrust suit and the lack of progress of congressional legislation. Consumer advocates were pleased with low phone rates but complained about delays and high costs of new products and services. And in the federal government, lawyers, regulators, and legislators were jockeying to become final arbiters of national telecommunications policy.

On January 8, 1982, the situation changed dramatically. AT&T and the U.S. Department of Justice announced agreement to settle the criminal antitrust suit out of court with a new consent decree. The distinction between information transmission and information services was finally abandoned. In exchange for nullification of the antitrust case and deregulation in major national and international markets, AT&T agreed to divest its twenty-two operating companies, and regulated and deregulated market opportunities were opened to the BOCs. (See figures 8–1 and 8–2.)

Most industry observers greeted the announcement optimistically. They expected a flurry of new products as a result of increased

---

The 1982 consent decree vacated the substantive provisions of the 1956 consent decree and substituted new requirements, including the following:

1. AT&T must divest itself of all twenty-two of its wholly or majority owned operating companies.

2. Prior to divestiture, these companies were to be reorganized so as to offer only exchange telecommunications service and not toll service or customer premises equipment.

3. Upon divestiture, the operating companies would be strictly limited in their business operations to exchange telecommunications service, exchange access service, information access service, and other "natural-monopoly" services regulated by tariff.

4. Upon divestiture, AT&T would be freed from the restrictions of the 1956 consent decree, which, in general, had limited it to the offering of common carrier communications services and confined Western Electric to the manufacture and sale of products used in connection with such service.

Source: "AT&T Settlement," in Oscar H. Gandy Jr., Paul Espinosa, and Janusz A. Ordover, eds., *Proceedings from the Tenth Annual Telecommunications Policy Research Conference.* (Norwood, N.J.: Ablex Publishing Corporation, 1983), p. 253.

Figure 8–1. *Terms of the 1982 Consent Decree*

market competition. Financial analysts viewed divestiture as an opportunity for a "big, powerful company, with tremendous strength and resources" to end its dormancy and break free."[6] More skeptical experts foresaw the costs and losses of splitting up "one of the best managed companies in the world."[7]

The consent decree resolved CI-II's ambiguities by dissolving the artificial line between data processing and communications and by rejecting the natural-monopoly model on which the telecommunications service industry had rested. Both specialty and regional networks were developing that would now compete with AT&T to carry long-distance calls. Large companies could bypass the public system in favor of their own networks, which would interconnect with the public network. Communications capacity became a commodity that could be bought and resold, with profits generated by providing information that flowed through the network and by transmitting signal information. The telephone system itself took on a new definition. It had the potential to become computerized and

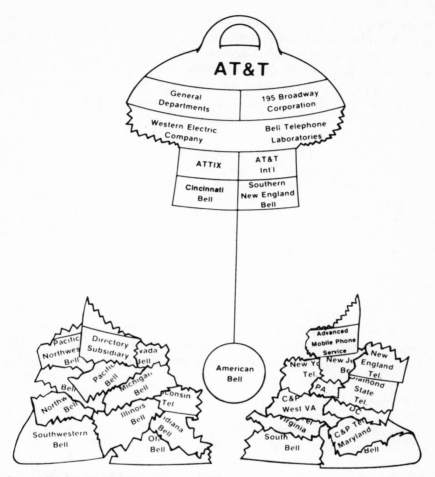

Source: George H. Bolling, *AT&T, Aftermath of Antitrust* (Washington, D.C.: National Defense University Press, 1983). Reproduction courtesy of National Defense University Press.

Figure 8–2. *Impacts of Divestiture on the AT&T Corporate Structure, 1984*

to be used to convey computer data, electronic mail, and video images in addition to voice communication.[8]

Chairman Brown recognized the settlement's scope in an internal report where he noted the difficulties involved in balancing consumers, share owners, employees, and national defense interests in managing "that unique natural resource, the best communications system in the world." He went on to say:

> I am confident that we have chosen the right course, although it is most assuredly not the outcome which we have so conscientiously sought. . . . This agreement confirms the central elements of what we believe to be national policy and disposes of debilitating uncertainties which have delayed investment decisions, inhibited innovation, and threatened both the equity of our share owners and the future of our employees.[9]

Within days of the settlement, AT&T placed advertisements in major newspapers and national periodicals explaining corporate views on its restructuring and the associated settlement. Within weeks, Brown announced the "realignment" plans that had already been formulated. Roles of the highest executives in the office of the chairman were redefined, and a management regrouping occurred. Brown stated that he, President William Ellinghaus, and Vice-Chairman James Olson would

> now devote themselves as a group to corporate strategy, resource allocation, and critical issues, although each will exercise oversight with respect to discrete sectors of the business. Ellinghaus . . . will be concerned with current operating matters in the existing Bell System. In addition, he will deal with matters involving future AT&T network organization and operations, prospective operating company centralized staff functions, and regulatory matters. Olson will be concerned with the organization and operation of AT&T's fully separated subsidiary, AT&T International, public affairs, human resources, labor relations, Western Electric, Bell Laboratories, and the 195 Broadway Corporation.[10]

The normal operating duties of the traditional general departments were divided among five new executive vice-presidents. At the same time, Chairman Brown appointed six "top-level study groups" consisting of senior AT&T staff and officers of the BOCs to direct key areas of planning for the operating companies. These groups were to examine such matters as the redrawing of exchange boundaries, the centralization of staff, the resolution of personnel issues, the design of new corporate structures, the assignment of assets, and the determination of network access charges for AT&T in the competitive environment.

AT&T subsequently reorganized into a new structure (see figure 8–3). The largest component of the new organization was AT&T Communications as the heir of Long Lines and provider of long-distance telephone service. The second major piece, AT&T Tech-

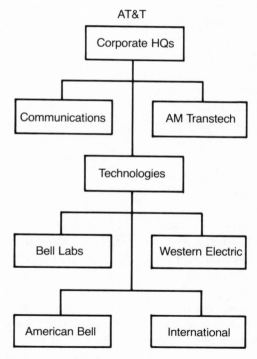

Reproduction courtesy of AT&T, 1986.

Figure 8–3. *AT&T Corporate Structure, Post-divestiture*

nologies, included Bell Labs and Western Electric, which initially remained intact. AT&T Technologies also featured a new unit, AT&T International, to explore market opportunities overseas. A new stockholder communications organization, American Transtech, also reported directly to corporate headquarters.

AT&T Technologies included another major entity, the arm's-length subsidiary created under CI-II. Through American Bell, AT&T could compete in the unregulated data-processing and computer markets. Forced to separate its board of directors, books, and accounts from those of the parent corporation, American Bell was also barred from owning or constructing transmission facilities. Common ownership was not permitted between the parent and subsidiary organizations. CI-II continued in force to prevent revenues and information gained in regulated activities from cross-subsidizing and supporting American Bell's operations.

In April, the twenty-two operating companies were gathered into seven regional companies and continued to provide regulated local telecommunications and exchange access services (see figure 8–4). In August, Judge Greene issued his verdict on the settlement, the Modification of Final Judgment (MFJ). Under its terms, all assets and liabilities related to local telephone service, long-distance service within certain zones, and the publication of telephone directories were to be under the regional holding companies' control. Each region was further carved into geographical units known as local access and transport areas (LATAs). The operating companies were forbidden to carry traffic between LATAs (even in their territories), as that business was reserved for long-distance carriers such as AT&T, MCI, and GTE Sprint. Otherwise, the regional operating companies were completely independent and autonomous, with their own self-chosen names and corporate identities. They were also permitted to pursue deregulated business opportunities on a case-by-case basis.

AT&T retained responsibility for intrastate, interexchange operations (long-distance services that crossed the LATA boundaries). The company's access to the divested local exchange companies followed the same terms as other long-distance carriers. AT&T retained ownership of customer premises equipment and the devel-

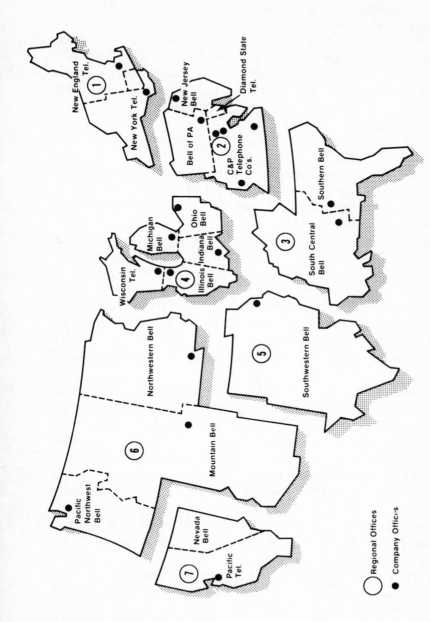

Source: George H. Bolling, *AT&T: Aftermath of Antitrust* (Washington, D.C.: National Defense University Press, 1983). Reproduction courtesy of National Defense University Press.

Figure 8–4. *Bell Operating Companies and Parent Regions, 1984*

opment, manufacture, sale, and leasing of telephone and other telecommunications equipment.[11]

At divestiture, on January 1, 1984, some $80 billion in current assets would be redistributed. In fairness to shareholders, ten "old" AT&T stocks were tradable for ten "new" AT&T stocks plus one share in each of the seven regional holding companies (post-divestiture).

Reactions and Responses

The most intense focus of media coverage was on divestiture's impact on telephone rates, but the chairman of a local Bell company moaned that divestiture was like "taking apart a 747 in midair and making sure it keeps flying."[12]

Other observers remarked on the managerial challenges facing both AT&T and the fledgling regional operating companies. *Fortune* magazine realized that "motivating former monopolists required vast changes in the way executives were assessed and rewarded,"[13] but Bell system managers had been adapting to competition for years. Now the operating companies felt fairly confident. On average, each regional had roughly $17 billion in assets, and territories ranging from two to fourteen states.[14] The field seemed wide open.

The operating companies continued to sell products to business users, but soon familiar questions began to surface. Should a regional operating company selling equipment or deregulated products be allowed to derive special pricing benefits from its relationship with the monopoly phone operation? What about market information to which the monopoly business had privileged access? Should the regulated side of the business tell the unregulated side's sales department when a corporate customer's call volume goes up and he looks like a good prospect for an electronic switchboard? What equipment should the companies sell and to which markets?

Pacific Bell, one of the new operating companies, concentrated on protecting its local network and profits by asking the state legislature for an outright ban on intra-LATA competition. Bypass continued to threaten them; what happened to a regulated player if a large telephone user developed its own private transmission network? As technological developments abounded, operating companies could no longer count on the high-volume business user revenues. Indeed, the same old problem of cream skimming seemed to threaten not the Bell System, but the divested Bell operating companies.

One potential new competitor to the regions was AT&T. Eager to develop new business, AT&T was moving into the private big-user communications market. The executive vice-president of AT&T heading the long-distance operations mentioned that decisions on bypassing the local companies depended on comparison price shopping,[15] although he knew well that the BOC operating company access charges (the price of an outside player's hookup into the old Bell network) and subsequent service pricing were still dependent on the state regulatory process.

For their part, while providing local phone services, the BOCs began to explore opportunities in nonregulated markets. The president of Pacific Bell, commenting that "new ventures are not the answer to a maiden's prayer," noted that over the past ten years only 20 percent of their earnings had derived from new businesses.[16] Northwestern Bell almost immediately contemplated expanding its directory business into areas outside its region. Proposed phone use to monitor oil production from remote wells didn't take off, but mobile phone service was developing quickly at Ameritech. Yet with the FCC granting franchises in each city on the basis of applications, price wars were anticipated among the many competitors. Few markets had the stability and security that regulation had traditionally afforded.

Looking Back

With divestiture, industry competition was expected to shift from courtrooms to the marketplace, but Congress was still grappling with decisions about possible subsidies to ensure that everyone could still afford phone service. Debates over access charges dominated industry battles between regulatory bodies, academicians, and the private sector. At the operating companies, concern was directed toward the dividends that shareholders were soon supposed to receive.

AT&T's continued regulatory struggle with the government was viewed by the media as "partly of its own making," but in some ways the conflict emphasized the inherent problems of the regulatory process in accommodating technological change. *Fortune* magazine wrote:

> If the leaders thought they knew what was best for the customer and resisted, to the point of anticompetitiveness, rival efforts to develop new approaches, [then] the antitrust settlement deliberately altered the nation's telephone system in a way that will force the phone company to respond quickly to customers' needs or lose their business.[17]

The statement underscored the operating problems faced by all industry players, particularly as market boundaries continued to change. Still carrying the bulk of the national long-distance network, AT&T faced erosion of this once secure market by aggressively priced competitors. In response to the threat, repricing experiments had begun along with incentive purchasing plans.

The global consequences of divestiture were also becoming apparent. Indeed, in the spring of 1985, FCC Chairman Mark Fowler pointed out that "in the international area, we've got to continue to foster competition . . . which is vital to the ability of American companies to compete effectively internationally."[18] Fowler's views may shed light on some motives behind the divestiture agreement; in some respects, it was an attempt to unleash a national champion in the global telecommunications wars. Indeed, international competition escalated as AT&T vigorously encouraged use of its international long-distance services. AT&T International established numerous joint ventures in its new product lines and looked toward recently deregulated markets as potential areas in which to offer technical, management, and supplier services.

For the consumer, the break up offered new and bewildering choices about which long-distance carrier to choose or what type of communications equipment to buy. For many businesses, however, telecommunications represented one piece of their value-added chain. Thus, as "the highway of the information age," the telephone system and the evolving industry structure affected the competitiveness of most businesses. New products continued to saturate the market, as did start-up ventures and collaborative investing. Despite local service cost increases, opponents of regulation continued to support divestiture. On the other hand, some consumers claimed that "What's needed is a little bit of regulation now to spread the benefits of competition more equitably."[19] Senator Barry Goldwater, however, perhaps best recognized the industry's vulnerability point when he observed: "I don't think I see a light at the end of the tunnel. What if one day AT&T said, 'To hell with it,' and blew up that big switchboard they have in Northern New Jersey?"[20]

9

Recasting Bell

When the 1982 consent decree settled the seven-year-old antitrust case against the Bell System, public reaction was mixed but generally skeptical. It was difficult to comprehend the magnitude of the event or its eventual impact. An independent telephone company chairman commented: "It is the dumbest thing that has ever been done. You don't have to break up the only functioning organization in the country to spur innovation."[21] Many large-account business users, however, had already begun to purchase alternative communications systems, thereby bypassing the Bell System. Residential customers anticipated rising phone rates in the absence of government protection, and it was unclear what innovations or new kinds of costs the new industry environment would bring.

Although AT&T had helped craft the consent decree, the company now faced a new challenge: What kind of organization would be successful in the new environment? The old AT&T had gained the public's trust, and top management emphasized the need to preserve that heritage. As Chairman Brown put it in a message to his employees:

> There is no "master plan" on file. . . . All of you will be kept informed as the planning takes shape. And many of you will have key roles in shaping various aspects of it. Meantime, your work goes on. In time, it will be structured differently—under different umbrellas—but it will be the same work, and it will be done by the same people who are doing it now for some time to come.

He concluded with a view of the future:

> You were selected for your present jobs because you were consid-
> ered to be the best. In the future, as in the past—but especially
> over the next several years as we adapt our new structures to the
> needs of the nation and the demands of the marketplace—we can
> settle for no less than the best.[22]

On that note, AT&T began the laborious task of planning once
more for major restructuring.

Managing the Transition

AT&T's first task was to comply with the consent decree and later
with Judge Greene's Modification of Final Judgment. During the
period between the announcement of the settlement and the divestiture, AT&T considered several strategies for change. The company
began the process of restructuring by reassigning headquarters staff
and dividing operations into regulated and deregulated categories.
A small corporate staff would provide broad governance, administration, strategic direction, financial control, and general policy for
the two branches, both of which would operate with a great deal
of autonomy.

In April 1982 a personnel subcommittee developed eleven recommendations dealing with issues such as affirmative action in hiring and retraining methods for older employees. It was the company's desire to retrain people rather than to redefine positions:

> Force imbalances will be addressed by movement of people be-
> tween entities, attrition, and other existing procedures for man-
> aging imbalances. Any imbalance should be resolved using exist-
> ing procedures before the transfer of functions wherever possible.
> Any remaining force imbalances will transfer with the work func-
> tion. Where work functions are split, force imbalances will be
> shared proportionately.[23]

By October 1982, general information and staffing policies
were distributed to all concerned department heads, assistant vice-

presidents, and directors. It was noted that to coordinate the many personnel shifts fairly, consistently, and smoothly in the coming months, open communication between managers and employees was essential. Each department was encouraged to organize informational forums so that "employees could have a sense of what the future was likely to bring."[24]

Chairman Brown described some key management challenges to the organization:

> Much remains to be done before our reorganization plan will be complete and before organizations can start to be realigned and individual assignments can be made. Work done so far in some parts of the Bell System indicates that a high percentage of assignment preferences can be accommodated and the needs of the business, which must of course prevail, can be met.

He also made a promise:

> As detailed decisions are made that affect Bell System people, I pledge that you will be informed promptly and on an individual basis about how you will be affected. You deserve nothing less.[25]

In the Bell System's traditional environment, low-cost installation, maintenance, and service had been management priorities. The deregulated environment, however, called for aggressive management and marketing, and AT&T stepped up efforts to develop those capabilities. New skills were needed at all levels within the organization. How could the company motivate the employees who stayed on? Employee loyalty and (in effect) lifetime employment commitments presented problems in a rapidly changing industry environment. Could the company continue to rely on a tradition of promoting from within to provide the managers it needed? Could traditional methods of decision making be applied in an industry where it was crucial to respond quickly to changing markets? How could the company transform an order taker into a salesmen, a bureaucrat into an entrepreneur, or a quiet middle manager into a risk taker and a leader?

The centralized organizational structure was unnecessary now that national network coordination no longer had to be maintained. The corporation could now produce and market computer hardware, software, and value-added services both domestically and overseas. Strategic planning became vital, as did the selection of managers who were comfortable working in an intense, competitive environment. As the company's priorities changed, "subsidiaries became holding companies, clients became competitors, colleagues became antagonists, subordinates became peers, and cooperative followers became rebels."[26]

AT&T set about reducing the general departments staff from almost 13,000 employees to fewer than 2,000. Although the downsizing effort was euphemistically dubbed "functional realignment," 2,000 people were transferred to American Bell. Despite extensive planning, job negotiations, and a hiring freeze, the transition was tense, for 12,430 people were eventually reassigned. AT&T Communications absorbed nearly half (5,800) of the former headquarters staff, and approximately 2,000 remained in the new corporate headquarters unit. Twenty-four hundred people were transferred to the BOC central staff (Bell Communications Research); another 1,000 joined the newly formed American Transtech Corporation, the stockholder communications subsidiary. Close to 900 moved to a new real estate subsidiary, the Resource Management Company.[27]

An internal study of the divestiture's impact commented on the stress resulting from these changes:

> There was an almost overwhelming concern among employees . . . regarding AT&T's ability to continue to provide high-quality service, given the demise of end-to-end service caused by the MFJ. . . . Employees tended to feel less secure about their jobs . . . and about their career opportunities . . . [and] wondered about AT&T's ability to compete, given the newness of the competitive environment and the remnant regulatory constraints still imposed.[28]

Anxieties surfaced as employees publicly shared that "we only agreed to divestiture because it was the better of a number of worse alternatives."[29] An internal survey asking employees to describe their feelings about the divestiture brought out still more frustrations. One employee felt "angry, sad, a little scared about my future. Divestiture was a triumph of lawyers, bureaucrats, and financial manipulators over producers and servers." Wrote another:

> I felt I had gone through a divorce that neither my wife nor my children wanted. It was forced upon us by some very powerful outside force and I could not control the outcome. It was like waking up in familiar surroundings (your home) but your family and all you held dear was missing.[30]

Chairman Brown responded to employees' concerns about the future by recalling the traditional AT&T service ethic that had always bonded the corporation. In a special edition of the AT&T management reports, he sounded an optimistic note:

> We have the human talent. We have the engineering and scientific resources. We are gaining the marketing skills and experience. We have our pride—we are not accustomed to being second best. . . . The future I see is an exciting and exhilarating time—both for the operating companies and for the AT&T entities. It is a time for establishing new goals, charting new strategies that look to the future rather than to the past.[31]

The means for instilling this sense of "old" purpose in a "new" company were both manifold and intensive. Using videotapes, management answered employees' questions about divestiture. Company publications featured articles explaining the "new" AT&T's mission in a reassuring light, and outside speakers shared their own views of the changes. The corporation's open admission of the transition problems did generate a sympathetic public response. Indeed, some comments from concerned customers provided valuable market information as AT&T set about formulating its new competitive strategy.

Management seminars trained 800 executives for the competitive telecommunications environment; their leadership then helped reorient the rest of the organization. Some parts of the company began formally recognizing employees' achievement in demonstrating competitive behavior, and rewards were given for outstanding marketing ideas or a high sales volume. Gradually a new culture began to form around competitive values.

With a new headquarters organization planned, AT&T next turned to the specific structural changes required for success in the new environment. The major divisions of the company became AT&T Communications, the direct descendant of the old Long Lines organization, and AT&T Technologies, whose responsibilities included Western Electric, Bell Labs, and—separated by the arm's-length requirements of CI-II—American Bell.

AT&T Communications

The company's plan for AT&T Communications was to make of it an entity that would merge and manage all the regulated segments of the post-divestiture organization. Although its business (regulated long-distance communications) remained essentially unchanged, some managers worried that the maturity of the close-knit regulated division would inhibit its integration with the newly competitive AT&T divisions. The task of integrating people and jobs from twenty-two Bell companies and seventeen departments of AT&T headquarters became more difficult, with conflicting attitudes and values about performance.

Despite these problems, however, AT&T Communications quickly launched an aggressive marketing campaign. The company attempted to retain customers through the direct mail "Opportunity Calling" incentive program. Long-distance discounts were offered through merchandise credits, and companies whose products and services were thereby exposed to AT&T customers absorbed the cost of the discounts. Operators began encouraging callers not to hang up so quickly.[32] One operator even encouraged callers to make person-to-person calls, as it brought in more revenue. Aware of her newly defined role, she said, "In a way, we're drumming up business."[33] Although some observers viewed the new program as an illustration of how AT&T was struggling to market a service that was once its birthright, the early results of "Opportunity Calling" were promising.

AT&T Technologies

AT&T Technologies was developed as an umbrella organization for AT&T Technology Systems (which included the parts of the old Western Electric that made computer and electronics products); Bell Labs; and three units that produced and sold consumer telephone products, international telephone service, and switching equipment for other telephone companies. The umbrella organization also included American Bell, the fully separated subsidiary required by CI-II.

AT&T Technologies was intended to oversee and coordinate these deregulated businesses. But the traditional consensus decision-making process involving AT&T headquarters engineering, Bell Labs, and Western Electric proved inadequate to meet the needs of the competitive marketplace. The traditional process was too slow, too cumbersome, and too diffuse to stay abreast of industry changes. Thus AT&T designed these subsidiaries as profit centers with simple executive accountability. Each unit was expected to develop its own marketing capabilities, shorten product development cycles, plan the release of future product lines, and create its own distribution systems—all within cost- and time-efficient guidelines.

Prior to divestiture, Western Electric had been dependent on the operating companies for 90 percent of its sales; in 1982 total purchases were approximately $12.4 billion. After divestiture, the operating companies could buy equipment in the open market, and AT&T's manufacturing arm experienced an "unexpected" loss of market share in telephone equipment sales. Western Electric responded to its changed circumstances by organizing along lines of business, and managers were encouraged to stretch their authority across various functions in order to pull together the effort needed to get a product to market. In addition to continuing to sell products ranging from central office switches to consumer telephones, Western expanded production into sales of semiconductors and computer hardware and software, and considered such new areas as medical equipment.

Despite its ambitious hopes, Western Electric faced serious obstacles at the start: as most of its sales had previously gone to its regulated affiliates, it retained a minuscule sales force for a company its size. Moreover, its products were built for durability in the era when telephones lasted for twenty-five years. Concerned about prices, however, consumers of the 1980s increasingly turned to lower-cost telephones. Many observers believed that with overengineered equipment, outmoded factories, and high-paid union labor, Western Electric would suffer in competition.

In 1983 Western Electric announced the closing of several of its older plants employing 11,000 workers, and Donald Procknow, president of the subsidiary, expected such "resizing" to continue. In the preceding forty months the company had cut some 40,000 jobs from its payroll. Western also acted aggressively to enter new markets. In 1983 it acquired an Irish communications equipment manufacturer in an attempt to crack the European market. This effort fizzled, however, because "the orders just weren't there," and AT&T closed one of the Irish company's two factories.[34]

In December 1983, AT&T headquarters decided to dissolve the Western Electric company formally, spreading the giant organization's people and plants among other divisions of the new AT&T. AT&T Technologies assumed Western Electric's corporate charter along with its financial obligations and other commitments. "We could have chosen to call this new enterprise Western Electric," said Chairman Brown, [but] "We chose instead to put all our resources and reputation behind the AT&T name." Charles Myers, an industrial organization expert at the Massachusetts Institute of Technology, saw the move as "the end of an era, of a company known for its forward-looking management and employee relations."[35]

Bell Labs, the research arm of the old AT&T, felt the effects of divestiture quickly. Nearly 7,000 of the 26,000 product development employees were transferred. Although 4,000 of them left for similar positions at AT&T Information Systems (ATTIS), the remainder moved to the Central Services Organization, the planning and development group for the divested operating companies. Roughly 1,500 other employees left the company through attrition. There was concern at the Labs that financial support would slacken compared to the predivestiture era; but although the 1984 budget shrank $1.5 billion, the 25 percent reduction roughly matched the staff reduction of about 30 percent.[36]

Before divestiture, Bell Labs' basic research activities provided two major payoffs: new knowledge that led to advanced telecommunications services, and new knowledge that produced patents and ideas used by outside companies. AT&T vice-chairman James Olson felt that "there is no reason for anyone at Bell Labs to be concerned about the future." Soloman Buchsbaum, executive vice-president for customer systems at Bell Labs, addressed the issue more directly: "Charlie Brown doesn't pay for research because he likes Arno Penzias (the Labs' head of research) or because AT&T is a good citizen. He pays for it because research is a good investment."[37]

The demands of the marketplace eventually altered Bell Labs' work. According to Barry Levine, a physicist heading the optical electronics research department: "We used to need inventions for other reasons, such as to exchange licenses. Now we need inventions because we need products."[38] The divestiture agreement also limited AT&T's proprietary rights to products coming from the Labs. For example, the Labs were required to provide regional operating companies with technical information and, until September 1987, to assist AT&T competitors as they plugged into operating company network systems.

Although the new workplace set stricter guidelines on research projects, the Labs had traditionally been a model for the management of basic research, and AT&T benefited from that labor through the years. Now, however, research emphasized improvements in operations systems and network planning, electronics technology, telephone switching systems, computer systems, and military telecommunications needs. Applying the research division's work to the competitive environment posed fewer threats than in the corporation's counterpart divisions, but one group did feel the impact of competitive change: the small but prestigious economics research group, part of whose job was to help the local companies in regulatory matters, was disbanded.

From American Bell to AT&T Information Systems

To comply with CI-II, AT&T had established a separate subsidiary, American Bell, in January 1983. This new subsidiary, representing AT&T's first thrust into deregulated business, was expected to become a power in office automation. Problems appeared almost immediately, however. American Bell's first product, a data communications network known as Net 1, had to be renamed Net 1000 when it was found that another company had already claimed the brand name. With 28,000 employees and no existing customers, the new company found its difficulties further compounded by product shortages. Judge Greene's decision to ban AT&T's use of the "Bell" name necessitated renaming the unit AT&T Information Systems (ATTIS) as well as developing a new corporate logo (see figure 9–1).

Before divestiture, about 85 percent of the old AT&T staff, including most of Arch McGill's marketing organization, had requested assignments at American Bell or ATTIS.[39] In May 1983, however, pieces of ATTIS were shifted back into AT&T Technologies. Among the casualties of this change was McGill, who resigned when his responsibilities were eliminated in the change. Some reports had it that he had angered older Bell hands in his efforts to transform the company during the 1970s.[40]

In January 1985, ATTIS regrouped once more into three lines of business to market more directly: computer systems, large-

Reproduction courtesy of AT&T, 1986.

Figure 9–1. *New AT&T Corporate Logo*

business systems (for customers with more than eighty phones), and consumer and general business systems (for residences and businesses with fewer than eighty phones). Each line of business had its own product development, product management, marketing, and distribution teams, as well as its own sales force.[41]

Pressure to Downsize

In November 1983, AT&T offered early retirement packages to 13,000 employees. The packages applied to personnel at ATTIS and AT&T Communications, where both divisions were seeking to reduce their payrolls by a total of $500 million.[42] In both divisions, it was the transferred employees from Bell Long Lines who were the targets of the offers. A spokesperson for ATTIS said, "What we have as a result of the restructuring is a work force that is too large to compete effectively."[43]

The *New York Times* predicted that pink slips might be the New Year's gift for thousands of Bell people in the early months of 1984. Brooke Tunstall recalled the issues differently: "It seems that we went through a series of stages. The same stages you go through in adjusting to divorce or death—shock, anger, disbelief, sadness— and then there was a sort of buckling down to get past the shock." Dr. Joseph Crumrine, AT&T's medical director, said: "I don't think there's any doubt that people are uptight. The main thing is jobs. Are they going to have them and what are they going to be doing?"[44]

Stress experts were brought in to conduct seminars to alert employees to signs of tension and pressure throughout the changes. Everyone was anxious. One Bell phone store worker wondered aloud: "I've worked for years for Southern Bell and now I'm going to work for AT&T. Will AT&T love me? Will AT&T take care of me?" Her husband spoke about the pace of the new company: "There isn't a whole bunch of time for lunch. Some days there isn't a whole bunch of time to go to the bathroom. . . . We've had it. We're sick of the phone company."[45]

When Francis Giunta's twelve-and-a-half-year job as a central office technician was eliminated, he didn't want to leave the town he had lived in all his life. He said he would take any other

AT&T job in Dubuque, but there was none. For him, divestiture represented

> Chaos. One day the people told me one thing. Two days later, they'd be told another thing. People are jockeying and shuffling for position, trying to find out where they can get the most job security. The way we were trained at Bell, there was just one way to do everything. . . . If you didn't know how to wipe your hands, you looked it up in the book. Now there isn't one right answer.

He added:

> Morale has dropped off. It's hard to feel that you're important and that you really matter in a world as big as the Bell system. You're like a little cog in a big machine. That comes out more at a time like this. How much does each one of us matter?[46]

Some employees welcomed the changes. "Now we're in the driver's seat," said Judith Amendola, a planner who left New York Telephone to work for its new regional holding company. "We set strategy for our own future. When I write a report and send it up the line, I can see that it's having impact."[47] But a Southern Bell employee who was singled out for a job transfer "felt extremely rejected" and stayed home from work for days. Although the transfer was a promotion, it apparently was not perceived as one.[48]

As January 1, 1984, arrived, employees had to face new relationships with many of their former colleagues. When AT&T Technologies personnel went to negotiate supply contracts with the seven operating companies, it "was like the peace talks for the Vietnam War," according to James Edwards, vice-president for marketing development. Relocations had placed operating company employees in the sales unit of ATTIS, and it was a sharp environmental contrast to their previous jobs. Work loads increased and became more demanding, and only 50 to 70 percent of their salary was guaranteed, the rest contingent on meeting sales quotas. "Two of the twenty-three transferees quit, one of the eight outsiders hired since didn't make it, and another employee is almost out," a marketing manager noted, and many people have been working nights and weekends, seeing many more accounts and really selling instead of just taking orders.[49]

Divestiture provided a prime case study for two psychologists interested in testing executive stress resistance. They discovered that "hardiness" was the key personality trait that helped employees adapt to the competitive challenge. Many of the 259 executives in the researchers' original AT&T sample retired early or moved to other companies, but the 87 who stayed at Illinois Bell and remained in the study saw themselves as more involved in their work because of the divestiture. They felt more support from upper management and believed that the company was becoming more innovative. One of them said: "It used to be pretty routine work, boring at times. Now, every day is a different day."

By contrast, those who were low in "hardiness" felt that their bosses were not giving them any support and complained about the constant changes in policy. One of these executives explained that he didn't let the changes bother him because "I just play it cool. I'm just waiting to retire." "How soon will you retire?" the psychologist asked. "In five years," the man replied.[50]

In August 1984, salaries were frozen through 1985 for 114,000 management-level employees, roughly one-third of AT&T's work force.[51] The move was expected to save AT&T $184 million and was viewed as the first of its kind in modern times (outside of government-influenced pay freezes). The company's bonus incentive programs and commission levels for sales personnel were left unchanged. Three weeks later the company officially announced plans to eliminate 11,000 jobs by the end of the year, which included eliminating 6,000 positions in information systems, 2,000 in consumer products, 2,000 in network systems, 1,100 in staff organization, and 150 administrative positions. The company planned to "minimize layoffs by relocating some employees and offering voluntary retirement and income protection" to others.[52]

Industry analysts predicted more organizational turmoil ahead for the company before its problems would be contained.[53] AT&T was considered a major player in the $45 billion long-distance market but, by its own count, was losing 5,000 long-distance business and residential customers a day to competitors such as MCI and GTE Sprint. AT&T Technologies was barely profitable, and former

AT&T managers (all of whom claimed anonymity) said that at least part of the reason was an organizational structure that included too many divisions and too many layers of management.[54]

To help solve these problems, AT&T retained several prominent consulting firms while internal pep rallies were held to keep up employee morale and motivation. Further staffing cuts seemed essential, especially as AT&T was saddled with costs of $61 an hour to install and maintain products and equipment, compared to IBM's hourly rate of $33 and MCI's $28. Despite the assistance of early retirement programs and regular attrition and resignations (5,000 workers gone), AT&T fell far short of its need to trim close to 13,000 workers.

Labor

Among the foremost critics of the divestiture were the leaders of the Communications Workers of America (CWA), the union that had represented hundreds of thousands of workers in the Bell System. As part of the new settlement, AT&T had proposed dividing the company's pension plan into eight separate plans to cover the seven regional holding companies and one parent company, but the union objected. Traditionally, AT&T employees had been free to move within the Bell System while maintaining their full pensions, benefits, and rights. After divestiture, the union protested, some workers would lose their pension benefits if they moved from one Bell subsidiary to another.[55]

The union's contract was due to expire in early August 1983, and contract talks began in mid-May. The issues on the table quickly escalated to include bargaining issues, politics, a possible public backlash, and the role of automation in the industry. The CWA sought an annual 3 percent wage increase for workers, richer cost-of-living adjustments, improved job security provisions, and other benefits.[56] The structure of bargaining within the new Bell System dominated the talks, however. A more fractious relationship between telephone workers and their employers was anticipated as the union worried that the seven regional holding companies would press for company-by-company negotiations to keep down future labor costs. CWA president Glenn Watts commented on the changes wrought by competition: "I think there is a real likelihood there will be more labor strife in the next decade than there has been in the last ten years." Rex Reed, vice-president for labor relations at AT&T, claimed, "We don't think the future structure of bargaining is something we need to address now."[57]

Large increases in local telephone rates were expected with the end of traditional cross-subsidies, and union leaders feared that the public would blame the workers and their wages, not divestiture, for higher phone bills. One union spent $500,000 on advertising to counter such a response. Meanwhile, Reed stated that he needed to examine wages and benefits relative to the new competitive environment; he insisted he could not afford large salary increases. John Carroll, executive vice-president of the union, described AT&T's new persona: "They appear to have a different attitude toward their work force. They seem to have an attitude that because we're competitive, we need to change the whole way we do things."[58]

The CWA anxiously sought contractual changes designed to protect jobs as the company introduced new technology and dealt with competitive inroads. In August 1983, roughly 700,000 AT&T workers went on strike. The stakes were high for both sides. Concerned about costs and its competitive position, AT&T demanded freedom to implement cost-saving technologies and strove to keep employees' salaries within a tight budget. Eventually the company and the union compromised on an agreement calling for modest wage increases and other benefits. The *Wall Street Journal* opined that the contract "enables economic survival," but many workers dissented, claiming that they were paying the price for the necessary productivity improvements and were sacrificing the chance for other personal gains down the road.[59]

In March 1984, 100 workers left ATTIS rather than accept relocations. In the same month, however, AT&T and the CWA reestablished the quality-of-worklife program, "a commitment of management and union to support localized activities and experiments to increase employee participation in determining how to improve work."[60] The project was designed to cope with the problems that the competitive environment posed for AT&T and hoped to answer some questions, including: Would divestiture affect commitment? Would workers be "deskilled"? Would work be organized to allow broad learning, including problem-solving skills that are not made obsolete by change? In a monopoly that has been able to maintain high levels of job security, how would management deal with down-turns and technological unemployment?

New Strategies, New Problems

In 1984 AT&T faced continuing political battles over subsidies and access charges. The company fought bitterly to change the rate structures mandated for long-distance communications. As part of the Bell system reorganization, the FCC had decreed that residential customers should pay the local operating phone companies access charges on a per-month, per-line basis throughout 1984 ($2), 1985 ($3), and 1986 ($4). Businesses would pay $6 a month. These charges were supposed to reflect the "real" cost of local service, after subtracting a traditional "subsidy" from more profitable long-distance service. AT&T worked hard to drive home the subsidy argument; notably, its arguments were based on an internal costing method. Numerous state public utility commissions rejected the system outright as invalid, and competitive battles over rate determination continued between AT&T, the FCC, and other stakeholders.[61]

In April 1984 the company asked the government to remove the regulation of interstate telephone service in order "to let the company's prices and services be governed by market forces,"[62] and it cited competitive disadvantage as its qualification. In May the FCC ruled to cut AT&T's long-distance rates by 6.1 percent, the first rate decrease ordered in fourteen years. The reduction in AT&T's rates narrowed the gap between its charges and those of the discount long-distance competitors, although the *New York Times* reported that AT&T still controlled 94 percent of the long-distance market.[63]

Customers, however, would not benefit as greatly as expected; concurrent with the cutback, the FCC approved increases in access charges (based on multiple phone lines) and an approved charge for interstate directory assistance. "We welcome the commission's action," said an AT&T spokesman. "This is something we have wanted to do for a long time."[64] The day after the long-distance charges decreased, AT&T applied for depreciation accounting changes that, if approved, would lead to rate increases. The petition said that current FCC depreciation rules spread the cost of plant and equipment investment over too long a time, leaving the company at at disadvantage relative to its less-regulated competitors. If the company sped up that cost recovery, a 3 percent increase in company revenue would be required.[65] In September the FCC forbade AT&T and the former operating companies to bill customers more than $343 million for litigation and court costs in federal antitrust suits, and by January the FCC again ordered lowered long-distance rates.

Competition in long distance began to heat up throughout 1984. AT&T's rivals included MCI, GTE Sprint, and almost every independent phone company.[66] The CWA estimated that for every percentage point of market share lost by AT&T, 1,000 members' jobs were endangered. By November, AT&T publicly acknowledged market threats as it took on lower-quality competitors in its advertising. The famous Ma Bell ads that softly asked consumers to "Reach out and touch someone" went bare knuckle, stating, "When you play telephone, if you can't hear everything, that's part of the game. But when you pay for calls it's no fun."[67] Although the prime goal was to induce customers to choose AT&T's products and services over others, the *New York Times* saw the ads "aimed at boosting employee morale and stimulating interest on Wall Street."[68]

While AT&T Communications was lobbying for a favorable rate structure and displaying a new toughness in advertising, AT&T Technologies unveiled its new line of data-processing equipment. In March 1984 the company introduced six models of new personal computers designed to compete with IBM's offerings. Reviews were mixed, however. As one writer put it, AT&T seemed "merely an interesting challenger that still needs some seasoning before it can do battle with the champ."[69]

AT&T, determined to be a full-line supplier, made it clear that more hardware would be coming. In February 1984 AT&T agreed to joint ventures with Convergent Technologies and United Technologies to supplement its line of office automation products. AT&T also increased its international strength by joining with N.V. Philips, a Dutch electronics concern, and Ing. C. Olivetti and

Co., an Italian office equipment company. Subsequent deals signed in 1984 and 1985 included moves into the European markets with UNIX Europe, the development of the home video game market over telephone lines with Coleco, movements into the videotext business with Chemical Bank, and a 10 percent company purchase of Intermatics Inc., a software concern. ATTIS joined with Hewlett-Packard and Wang to produce interfaces that linked AT&T's data-processing equipment with other equipment in the market. Agreements with many vendors in trans-Atlantic fiber cable systems moved the company into the fast-paced world of high-speed data processing and digital transmission.

Product shortages and unmet deadlines caused significant problems, however, as did the persistent product orientation of senior management, who were unaccustomed to forecasting market demand and anticipating customer needs. For example, AT&T's manufacturing executives, failing to foresee the explosive demand for computer memory chips, canceled construction of a new chip plant in Florida. By the time the product was manufactured and delivered, a potential competitive advantage had been lost.

AT&T also squared off against IBM in software, where AT&T's UNIX operating system competed with the popular IBM PC-DOS. Which giant would control the standard that linked the various products of an information system? The answer lay in the future, although AT&T's early returns in 1984—$1.4 billion in net income, $1.25 per share—were considered discouraging (see table 9–1).[70]

To improve its orientation to the marketplace, AT&T began using a "competitive skills workshop" as an employee training tool in 1985. Said the division manager of education at AT&T Communications' Sales Marketing Education Center: "We needed to get a wealth of product and service information to the sales force, build the corporate culture for the new AT&T, and do it economically. So we built the National Teletraining Network."[71] Concurrently, the company worked on reducing the intensity of employee supervision to induce individual creativity and decision making, while hoping to streamline the internal chain of command.

Bob McCormack, a technician for ATTIS, noted the differences in his work. For sixteen years as a repairman going by the Ma Bell book, he drove a van with a ladder stuck on the roof, wore overalls,

Table 9–1

Selected AT&T Financial Data, 1984

(dollars in millions, except per share amounts)

	Post-divestiture[a]	Pre-divestiture			
	1984	1983	1982	1981	1980
For the year:					
Total operating revenues	$33,188	$ 70,319	$ 65,866	$ 58,655	$ 51,152
Total operating expenses	30,893	57,338	50,678	44,365	38,728
Income before extraordinary charge	1,370	5,747	7,279	6,823	5,967
Extraordinary charge—net of taxes	—	(5,498)	—	—	—
Net income	1,370	249	7,279	6,823	5,967
Preferred dividend requirements	112	127	142	146	150
Income applicable to common shares	$ 1,258	$ 122	$ 7,137	$ 6,677	$ 5,817
Earnings per common share (in dollars)	$ 1.25	$ .13	$ 8.40	$ 8.47	$ 8.04
Based on average shares outstanding (in millions)	1,010	937	850	788	724
Dividends declared per common share (in dollars)	$ 1.20	$ 5.85	$ 5.40	$ 5.40	$ 5.00
At end of year:					
Total assets	$39,827	$149,530	$148,186	$137,750	$125,553
Long-term debt including capital leases	$ 8,718	$ 44,810	$ 44,105	$ 43,877	$ 41,255
Preferred shares subject to mandatory redemption	$ 1,494	$ 1,523	$ 1,550	$ 1,563	$ 1,575
Convertible preferred shares subject to redemption	—	—	301	336	385
Other statistics for 1984:					
Current ratio	1.54				
Capital expenditures	$ 3,215				
Return on average common equity	9.48%				

Source: American Telephone and Telegraph Company and its subsidiaries, *Annual Report, 1984*. Reproduction courtesy of AT&T, 1986.

Note: On January 1, 1984, AT&T was required by court to divest those parts of the Bell System operating telephone companies that provided local exchange and exchange access services and printed directory advertising. As a consequence of divestiture, 1984 financial results are not comparable to those of prior years. This change is discussed in notes (A) and (B) to the financial statements.

[a]Because of divestiture, 1984 financial results are not comparable to prior years.

had tools slung around his waist, and went wherever his dispatcher told him to go. Now he dressed in slacks, button-down shirt, tie, and sport jacket; he drove a new station wagon and carried his tools in an attaché case. "Just like they do at IBM," he said proudly. Instead of going to do whatever job the dispatcher had next on the list for him, he had his own clients and could decide what jobs to tackle and in what order. "They call me Bob," he says. "I used to be just the telephone man wherever I went. It's made a heck of a difference."[72]

Raising the Stakes

In the first quarter of 1985, AT&T produced a 55.9 percent increase in earnings and had revenues of $8.3 billion.[73] In April GTE considered selling Sprint, its long-distance unit, because "it found the long-distance industry a hostile environment for AT&T's competitors."[74] In May MCI announced plans to spend about $400 million to expand its U.S. telecommunications network by adding optical-fiber routes, a move expected to increase MCI's transmission capacity by 80 percent.[75]

In 1983 Alvin von Auw, a vice-president at AT&T, had written that:

> It had soon become clear that the zealots for a Bell System "financially-driven and market-oriented" were no less committed to excellence in service performance than were the keepers of the business' traditional service icons.[76]

After the divestiture, AT&T hoped to blend that commitment to excellence with the aggressive management required by players in the highly competitive telecommunications industry. The stakes, however, continued to rise. In June 1985 IBM announced the intention to acquire a 16 percent holding in MCI, thereby adding communications capability to its formidable data-processing business. Randall Tobias, chairman and CEO of AT&T Communications, saw the new combination as increasing "what is already an enormously competitive situation."[77] Pressure on costs was becoming more intense, and AT&T became much more aggressive in its efforts to reduce personnel (see figure 9–2).

IF YOU ARE LOOKING FOR GOOD PEOPLE...

This is your chance to connect with some of the smartest, most capable and highly trained people in America today.

We have consolidated many of our operations recently. This move creates an opportunity for you and your company if you are looking for highly talented, skilled people.

Here is our number, 1-800-225-HIRE. Please call between 8am and 6pm, Monday through Friday, Eastern Time. We only ask for a minute of your time — or more, depending on your staffing needs. Tell us who you need to make your company run smoother or faster or further or better.

Please have ready all the information on numbers and types of openings, locations of various opportunities, salary ranges, contact names, addresses and telephone numbers.

We will get your requirements to some very special people in the following fields:

Engineering
Skilled Trades
Technical Support
Manufacturing
General Administrative

Our employees will contact you directly if they are interested in what you have to offer. We leave the rest in your — and their — capable hands.

It is direct, easy, free, quick — and our way of proving that we want the best for all our employees.

1-800-225-H I R E
MONDAY - FRIDAY 8AM - 6PM EASTERN TIME

AT&T

Reproduction courtesy of AT&T, 1986.

Figure 9–2. *AT&T Outplacement Advertisement*

AT&T's long-term ability to survive the new competitive rivalry would undoubtedly be determined in the marketplace. The company, however, greeted its new challenges enthusiastically. As its post-divestiture slogan boldly proclaimed, "The Future Is In Our Hands"—at last.

10
The Birth of U S WEST, Inc.

On a late July afternoon in 1984, Jack MacAllister, president and CEO of U S WEST, Inc., looked out from his office toward the west, to the Rocky Mountains beyond Englewood, Colorado, the site of the company's headquarters. Though the panorama was spectacular, MacAllister's thoughts lay elsewhere. Earlier in the day, he had received a copy of an opinion from Judge Harold H. Greene of the U.S. District Court in Washington, D.C., that apparently challenged the diversification strategies of U S WEST as well as the other six regional holding companies created by the breakup of the Bell System.

Thirty months earlier, when the historic consent decree between AT&T and the U.S. Department of Justice was announced, MacAllister had been president of Northwestern Bell, one of the twenty-two phone operating companies that AT&T agreed to divest. The following spring, AT&T chairman Charles L. Brown had named MacAllister as the head of the new regional holding company that would own Northwestern Bell, Mountain Bell, and Pacific Northwest Bell.

This new corporation, soon named U S WEST, quickly charted a distinctive strategy for its independent life, which began on January 1, 1984. U S WEST would not be modeled on the old AT&T, nor would it be merely a telephone company. Officers of the new company believed that the settlement of the antitrust suit had not put an end to the technological, competitive, and regulatory trends that had transformed the telecommunications industry in the prior decade. Rather, they believed that more changes were coming, and they intended to play a role in shaping them. U S WEST decided to

184 Chronicles of Corporate Change

press for still further deregulation of telecommunications and to take an aggressive stance in favor of more competition. The company created separate subsidiaries to compete in nonregulated businesses such as directory advertising, customer premises equipment, cellular telephone service, and telephone systems engineering. By the summer of 1984, U S WEST was also looking to enter additional markets through more new subsidiaries or acquisitions.

Now, however, Judge Greene—who had presided during the AT&T antitrust trial and who had himself approved the final terms of the divestiture in the Modification of Final Judgment (MFJ)—appeared to call this strategy into question. The judge was worried that the regional holding companies were acting in ways that ran contrary to the spirit, if not the letter, of the settlement. He outlined a series of conditions that he would apply in reviewing the companies' requests to enter new businesses, and announced that "the Court will not, for the present, grant waivers for activities whose total net revenues exceed 10 percent of the net revenues of the Regional Holding Company's revenues."

Although U S WEST's pending waiver petitions satisfied the judge's conditions, and its diversified interests accounted for far less than 10 percent of total revenues in 1984, Jack MacAllister worried about the long-term implications of the new opinion. How long would regulation and judicial oversight continue to constrain U S WEST's strategic plans?

Divestiture and Its Aftermath

When representatives of AT&T and the Justice Department met on January 8, 1982, to sign the consent decree terminating a seven-year-old criminal antitrust suit, they transformed the structure of the telecommunications industry. In a single stroke, the nation's richest company and largest private employer agreed to divest its ownership of twenty-two local exchange telephone companies, representing some $80 billion in assets and roughly 750,000 employees—all within eighteen months.

Analysts immediately hailed AT&T's action as a brilliant stroke. The company would retain what seemed to be its most attractive assets—its dominant role in long-distance transmission, and its research and manufacturing subsidiaries—while gaining access to high-growth markets that the regulators and the courts had long forbidden. At the same time, the company would lose its less-promising operating companies, which apparently faced a humdrum future as high-grade but low-growth public utilities.

At Northwestern Bell, Jack MacAllister and his top officers took a different view of the consent decree. They saw it as a halfway measure that left the operating companies in the same bind that had hampered AT&T for decades. "Regulation has never been able to stand in the way of technological change," MacAllister pointed out.

> The whole history of the Bell system shows what can happen. Even though AT&T was regulated, it got sued by everybody in the country, and it lost a substantial part of its business while its rivals used new technologies to compete. The consent decree doesn't change that. The so-called *natural monopoly* will continue to erode. In my view, the best way to protect our investment here is to be procompetitive, to get free of regulation as soon as possible.

Top leaders of Northwestern Bell, then, were more inclined to see opportunities than problems in the terms of the consent decree. No longer would they be at AT&T's beck and call, required to report to corporate staff in New York and New Jersey. No longer would they be expected to produce massive streams of information on everything from operators' average time of calls and other specific service measures to the details of investments in central office equipment for analysis back East. And no longer would they have to submit to AT&T's financial planning and control system, which had annually absorbed officers' time and energy. Potentially the company would be free to make its own strategic decisions, and to organize and manage itself as it saw fit.

The day after the announcement of the consent decree, MacAllister appointed a task force of Northwestern Bell managers to begin planning for the changes ahead. Immediate problems included communicating and explaining the consent decree to the company's 25,000 employees, long-range planning for Northwestern Bell's independent future, and working with AT&T and the court on the details of the divestiture itself. At the same time, AT&T's Chairman Brown appointed MacAllister to a study group of BOC presidents to plan for the restructuring of local telephone service.

Communicating the Changes

Although the highest officers of the Bell Operating Companies (BOCs) had at least some warning of the consent decree, its announcement fell like a bombshell throughout the Bell System. At Northwestern Bell, many employees were stunned. Some had spent their entire careers in the Bell system. Others were themselves children or grandchildren of people who had worked for the telephone company. Most had taken their jobs on the basis of assumptions and expectations that suddenly had become obsolete. Some employees hoped to move to AT&T after the breakup, whereas others preferred to stay in the familiar environment of Northwestern Bell. Most were confused and uncertain about what the future would bring.

Top officers immediately saw the need to stress positive aspects of the coming changes as well as continuities with the past. Since MacAllister had become president of Northwestern Bell in the mid-1970s, company programs and publications had portrayed the changes sweeping the telephone industry in upbeat terms of opportunity and challenge. One program, called "Willing the Future," had encouraged employees to consider how the company's traditional organization and management would have to change in a more competitive environment. Employees were exhorted to learn to live with greater uncertainty, to take risks, and to think as entrepreneurs. Also developed were programs to increase cost-consciousness and to shrink the company's managerial ranks and total employment.

Northwestern Bell's officers escalated these efforts early in 1982. In speeches, forums, videotapes, and employee newsletters, the officers explained the settlement carefully and patiently. But they also emphasized that the future would not bring a sharp break with the past. As MacAllister recalled:

Our own divestiture planning was essentially a continuation of the direction we had been taking since 1979, especially in downsizing the staff. My job was to get people ready for change as soon as possible. We knew change was coming, and that the environment was becoming more competitive. So we've been reducing the number of people on the payroll, especially in middle management—all levels of management. In 1979, 33,000 people worked at Northwestern Bell; by 1982, we were already down to 25,000.

In addition, we had been trying to drive decision making from the upper levels of management down to lower levels, where it would be closer to the market, to broaden spans of control, to force delegation of responsibility. If the job is too big for one manager to do by himself, he'll have to delegate.

Planning: From the Consent Decree to the MFJ

Dick McCormick, who was vice-president of network services at Northwestern Bell in 1982, described how analysts and managers reacted to the consent decree:

I would characterize the attitude of people on the outside like this: If the local Bell Operating Companies go out of business, that's O.K.; it's in the public interest if competitive market forces replace an obsolete monopoly. We'll just isolate and regulate the remaining natural monopoly and watch it shrink.

But that's not my attitude, and it's not the attitude of others here. From the operating companies' point of view, we want to be as creative and innovative as possible, to push our internal abilities and external constraints to the limit. We're now forced to look at the opportunities we have in the operating companies in a new light, and there are some very interesting possibilities—cellular mobile service, the digital office, fiber optics, packet switching, and more. Under the old copper-wire and mechanical-switch technology, the operating company would have the central office, the basic wire center, the local distribution network, and a lot of cable. But the new systems are capable of lots more. They're the key to this business.

One thing I've noticed—since January 8, there has been a phenomenal increase in the interest in strategic planning, especially in the local distribution business. People are trying to figure out how to make it profitable.

According to Larry Kappel, head of strategic planning at North-western Bell, the company began systematic planning for its future almost immediately:

> On January 9, Jack had a meeting to get people to work on what we could do with this, what kind of business to make it. I was convinced that planning around lines of business, which we had been working on for a while, would still work. We just had fewer lines of business to plan for. So I took out some of the stuff we had collected, and laid out an eight-step process to divestiture. It began with the identification of major issues left open—operator services, major suppliers, and so on—and ended with an effort to define what our lines of business would be. Along the way, we made efforts to understand the new environment, outlined competitive issues, rethought our mission, and set up planning teams for each line of business. We worked hard to have a well-planned corporate entity ready for divestiture.

The consent decree gave the Bell System a year and a half to get ready for divestiture. During that time, AT&T and each of the operating companies not only had to work out important unresolved issues and attend to thousands of details, but they also had to continue to operate the nationwide telephone system. Under such pressured conditions, AT&T's corporate staff—which had presided over major reorganizations of the Bell system three times in the previous decade, and which has been accustomed to supervising the operating company managements closely—took it on themselves to manage the divestiture planning process.

Almost immediately, however, Northwestern Bell began to act independently. Said MacAllister:

> We had been working to replace internal measurements of performance with an external focus. We had a big fight with AT&T on that one—it wanted to hang on to the old measures. The most strain between Northwestern Bell and AT&T came during the period from January 1982 to May 1982, and the issue was the mea-

surements. The AT&T staff was accustomed to dealing with all the issues. The divestiture process was very worrisome for them, in part because their own jobs were at stake. They also found it disquieting that they could no longer tell us what to do.

At the same time that it was asserting its independence from AT&T's staff direction, Northwestern Bell and other operating companies were contesting some terms of the divestiture settlement—the most important being the rights to the use of the Bell trademark, the control of directory services, and the ability of the BOCs to enter competitive telecommunications markets through separate subsidiaries. In the summer of 1982, Judge Greene ceded the rights to the Bell name to the operating companies and forbade AT&T to use it except for its subsidiary, Bell Telephone Laboratories. More serious problems for the operating companies centered around language in the consent decree that had given AT&T control of the lucrative Yellow Pages business and appeared to confine the BOCs to the local exchange business.

In August, Judge Greene issued his Modification of Final Judgment, which settled the terms of the divestiture at last. Citing concerns about the financial viability of the BOCs, the judge returned directory services to the operating companies and allowed them to "provide, but not manufacture, customer premises equipment." In addition, the MFJ created a loophole in the consent decree's provisions that had forbidden the BOCs to "provide any other product or service, except exchange telecommunications and exchange access services, that is not a natural monopoly service actually regulated by tariff." Judge Greene agreed to waive this restriction on a case-by-case basis, provided that the petitioning BOC could show that "there is no substantial possibility that it could use its monopoly power to impede competition in the market it seeks to enter."

The judge was silent about how long the court would retain jurisdiction over these matters, saying only that it would continue "for such further orders or directions as may be necessary or appropriate for the construction or carrying out of this Modification of Final Judgment, for the modification of any of the provisions hereof, for the enforcement of compliance herewith, and for the punishment of any violation hereof."[78] It was generally understood, however, that judicial oversight would continue at least until the BOCs fully implemented policies for equal exchange access—a process that might last several years.

The Formation of U S WEST

Shortly after the consent decree was announced, AT&T's Chairman Brown had appointed six study groups of company officers and BOC presidents to plan for divestiture. MacAllister served on the study group that investigated corporate structuring. In April 1982 Brown followed this study group's recommendations to organize the BOCs into seven regional holding companies with roughly similar financial characteristics. Northwestern Bell was grouped with Mountain Bell and Pacific Northwest Bell in a gigantic T-shaped territory that covered fourteen states between the Mississippi River and the Pacific Ocean, and from the Mexican to the Canadian borders. The new region would have total assets of $17 billion and total employment of nearly 80,000 people. Although some analysts worried that the region would face high costs because of its geographical spread and largely rural economy, the region also included high-growth areas in the Southwest and the Northwest and in metropolitan areas such as Minneapolis and Denver.

In May 1982 Brown put MacAllister in charge of planning for the region, whereupon MacAllister stepped aside as president of Northwestern Bell, and was succeeded by Dick McCormick. Upon his new appointment, MacAllister called a meeting to plan the new regional holding company. The presidents of the three BOCs in the region, along with one outside director from each company, joined MacAllister on this regional advisory board.

Before—and during—the first meeting, MacAllister had doodled his ideas about the new company on a single sheet of paper (see figure 10–1). These notes reflected important strategic choices MacAllister was mulling over: the new corporation would not be simply a telephone company; rather, it would be a diversified financial holding company run by a very small headquarters staff.

Although Judge Greene had not yet settled the terms of the MFJ, MacAllister argued that the new corporation should compete in nonregulated markets. His sketch of the company's organization

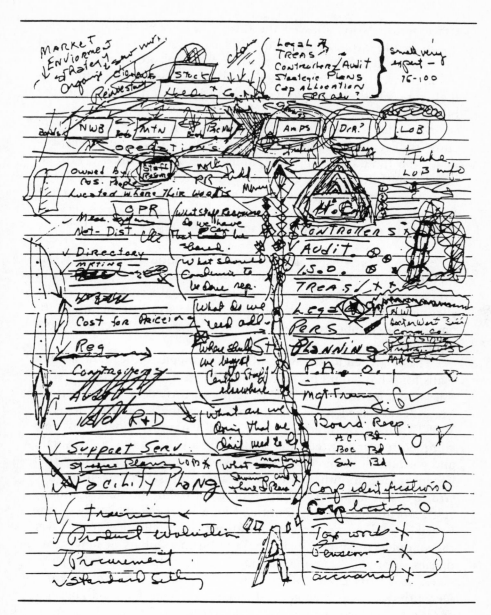

Figure 10–1. *MacAllister's Doodles, April–May 1982*

chart (figure 10–1) showed the three BOCs reporting to the corporate headquarters. Next to the BOCs on the chart, but separated
by a thickly drawn wedge, were three other subsidiaries for mobile
phone service, directory service (which, under the terms of the original consent decree, belonged to AT&T), and other lines of
business.

MacAllister also argued that the new company should not oc-
cupy itself with managing the telephone business. In his notes, be-
neath the three operating companies, MacAllister drew a box la-
beled "Staff Resources." The new holding company would not
provide staff support to the BOCs, as AT&T had done. Instead, the
BOCs themselves would be responsible for deciding which services
to share in common and for managing those services as they saw
fit.

Finally, MacAllister argued that the headquarters staff of the
holding company should be "small"—perhaps 75–100 people—and
"very expert." Management at this level would consist of six departments: legal, treasury, controller/audit, strategic planning, finance, and public relations. No line operating functions were
represented.

The board endorsed MacAllister's strategic and organizational
plans for what would become U S WEST at its first meeting.[79] With
this fundamental direction set, the board turned to other matters.
MacAllister asked it to become a nominating committee for U S
WEST's board of directors. "I wanted a national board, not one
confined to our fourteen states. But I also wanted the board small,
and with the directors in control of who joined," he said. The group
began to meet monthly to work on a mission statement, formulate
strategy, and approve key appointments to the holding company
staff. During the ensuing months, MacAllister relied heavily on the
board in making key strategic and organizational decisions. Over
the summer, the board evaluated the business plans of new subsidiaries to provide customer premises equipment and directory services, and considered other new ventures. In September Larry
DeMuth, who had been general counsel for Mountain Bell, became
executive vice-president and chief legal officer of U S WEST. At the
same time, Howard Doerr, chief financial officer at Northwestern

Bell, was appointed executive vice-president and chief financial officer.

While the board went about its work, MacAllister also appointed intercompany study teams to work on pressing issues in forming the new company. Task forces met to discuss policies for combining the treasury, network, and strategic planning functions of the BOCs. According to Larry Kappel, "The underlying question was, how do we put the three telephone companies together?" As he described it:

> I chaired the planning committee with my coordinates from Mountain Bell and Pacific Northwest Bell. Our job was to determine what kind of process would be used for planning. There was considerable apprehension about using lines of business as the basis of planning by the people from Mountain and PNB. So the regional planning process allowed for lines of business but didn't require them. We put together a generic planning process.

By the fall of 1982 U S WEST had decided to establish its headquarters in the Denver area and had filled out its officer team. The officers and the three BOC presidents spent three days together in November working on statements of basic mission and strategy, and defining roles for the staff and the subsidiaries. The group eventually adopted the following statement of corporate commitment: "The primary responsibility of the board of directors and employees of U S WEST is to create the highest possible value for our investors through long-term profit on investor's capital and by maximizing the growth of that capital." Said MacAllister:

> If there is a difference between what we were trying to do and what happened in the other six regions, it is in our view of the basic purpose of the holding company and its singular direction, with the end point being what's good for the shareholders. We're not here to manage operations; we're here to improve the value of the shareholder's investment through the selection of good strategies.
>
> Our statement of commitment is displayed in every U S WEST conference room, and it's printed on the back of every employees'

paycheck, including mine. This commitment to serving shareowners is the overriding consideration in every decision we make, and is the nucleus of our management philosophy, organizational structure, and vision of the future. More than anything else, they describe the character and content of our organization. They are also the basis for our claim that U S WEST is not a telephone company.

U S WEST's Strategy

In order to achieve the objective of providing the highest possible value for its investors, the officers and board of U S WEST agreed on three basic, long-range strategies: (1) to maintain a clear separation between regulated and unregulated businesses, (2) to press for further deregulation and equal terms of competition, and (3) to diversify into high-growth markets.

Separation

Establishing and maintaining a clear separation between regulated and unregulated businesses was intended to minimize the risk of antitrust litigation, to enhance chances of further deregulation of the Bell Operating Companies' activities, and to help obtain authorization from the Department of Justice and Judge Greene for U S WEST to enter new businesses not specifically authorized by the MFJ. With regard to antitrust litigation, Larry DeMuth said:

> If there is one lesson to learn from the immediate past, it's that we cannot use the telecommunications business to create an advantage for ourselves in competitive markets without being in real trouble. Those who forget the lessons of history are condemned to relive the past. And we in this region are not going to relive history—we are going to make history.

DeMuth also pointed out that clear separation would enable the company to insulate the profits of competitive businesses from use by regulators as a subsidy for telecommunications:

The law is clear. Only monopoly markets are properly subject to regulation. Only when you design your business to give the regulators access to your profits are those profits subject to regulatory capture. Of course, that design can be through inaction rather than deliberate action. But the fact remains that through a proper approach you can clearly effect a separation of profitable, competitive businesses from regulated businesses.

The Bell System was deliberately designed to be subject to regulation. The 1956 consent decree was interpreted to extend and expand that regulation, and the whole philosophy was to gain protection from competition. The law does not require that we be subject to regulation. Nor does it require us to hang onto our old concepts or our old ways of thinking. We can separate our lines of business, and we can capture the profitability of those competitive lines for the shareowner.

To implement the strategy of separation, each subsidiary was to have separate locations, a separate accounting system, a separate staff, and separate payrolls, including separate labor contracts where appropriate. No holding company officer was to serve in any capacity on the staffs or boards of directors of the Bell Operating Companies. In the company's view, these measures, backed up by an explicit top management philosophy supporting separation, were sufficient to assure that regulated resources would not be used against competitors of unregulated units.

This strategy also influenced U S WEST's relations with the other regional holding companies. The MFJ had authorized the seven regions to set up a central services organization "for the provision of engineering, administrative and other services which can most efficiently be provided on a centralized basis."[80] The central services organization was funded from assessments against the operating telephone companies, which in turn included these costs in their rate bases. U S WEST took the position that it could not sign the common ownership agreement as long as it contained provisions that afford the potential for requiring the company to fund anticompetitive activities. In the spring of 1984 MacAllister explained:

We are the only regional holding company that has not signed the shareholders agreement, which deals with the funding of *core* projects you must participate in, such as developing software updates for electronic offices. We may not sign it. We want to buy services we need, not others. We want the flexibility to opt out of any projects with potential for competitive conflicts. The way the agreement is now written, the vote of five other regions would obligate us to participate in such projects.

Deregulation and Competition

U S WEST's strategy of advocating deregulation and working toward equal competition in all aspects of its business rested on the belief that, sooner or later, all telecommunications markets would become competitive. By actively seeking to deregulate its telecommunications businesses, the new company hoped to get a head start on competition. "Let the marketplace decide," urged MacAllister. "The marketplace makes *better* decisions about price than regulators, and it makes them more *efficiently*."

U S WEST's attitudes toward regulation and competition also reflected the strategic role that Larry DeMuth played in the company. Unlike general counsels in most corporations, DeMuth took an active part in shaping U S WEST's strategy, as did lawyers in U S WEST's subsidiaries. As DeMuth described it:

The involvement of lawyers in strategic planning is holistic and continuous. There's nothing that goes on at U S WEST that doesn't involve the participation of lawyers. It's just as essential a function in strategic planning as finance. Everything depends on the law, and the lawyers are the theologians. In our case, the MFJ is like the Bible—it's subject to a lot of interpretation.

DeMuth's view of the MFJ was radically different from that of Judge Greene and many early analysts:

Regulation is irrelevant in an environment of competition. This is the Achilles heel of the consent decree. The MFJ did nothing to change the basic regulatory picture for the BOCs. It didn't simplify the regulatory environment, except insofar as it amputated their concerns about those portions of the business that were in a competitive environment. The MFJ was surgery—it separated the regulated side of the business from competition. But the whole thing is competition. Regulation is an anachronism in the industry. Some economists argue that there's still a natural monopoly left in the local exchange and that both regulation and antitrust law are needed. But even that is changing fast. Although we're portrayed as a rural region, the vast majority of our business is not in remote areas, where it is the subject of legitimate regulation. Most of our business is in urban areas, where competitive alternatives already exist. The only relevant issue is antitrust law, which is designed to regulate competition; the regulatory apparatus is designed to regulate monopoly, not competition.

That is essentially the whole predicate for our strategy. The visionary part of this job is figuring out how to resolve the tension between current reality and what we know the future has to be like.

Addressing U S WEST officers at a conference in June 1983, DeMuth elaborated:

Let's dispel the notion now that the MFJ says that we are relegated to being monopolists. It is true that the MFJ says that we can be in any business that is a natural monopoly as long as we proceed under tariff. But it never defines any business that is a natural monopoly, and interestingly, it does not say that provision of exchange telecommunications services and exchange access services are a natural monopoly.

The Bell telephone operating company subsidiaries and the other subsidiaries of U S WEST are *all* really competitive companies. We have the opportunity to separate certain lines of business at divestiture and immediately free those lines of business from regulation. It will take longer to free the profits of our operating companies from regulation, and the process will be more complex. . . . [But] freeing those profits from regulation is the objective.

Some managers at U S WEST argued that the other regions had failed to come to grips with the full implications of the consent decree and ongoing technological change. Said one:

The other companies may run the risk of antitrust suits in the way they're handling the competitive parts of their business. They're counting on the lines between regulated and competitive segments of the business being blurry. It's hard to see that they've learned anything from divestiture.

These companies are continuing to rely on regulation as a defense against competition. The new world we're living in is very threatening to many people. At the same time, the traditional culture and mind set in the Bell System remains very strong. The basic problem is that the Bell System didn't value profits highly. We knew we needed adequate earnings to attract capital and fund the growth of the system, but we were mainly concerned about service and the maintenance of our monopoly. Not everyone sees the need to change those values.

The other regional holding companies tend to view us as heretics. They're dedicated to the maintenance and expansion of the traditional regulated monopoly, while we're trying to hasten its end. The shareholders' agreement on the central services organization is essentially an attempt to maintain the core of the old monopoly. That's why we haven't signed it.

Diversification

The third major part of U S WEST's strategy was to diversify into markets where executives believed they could compete for a profit greater than that allowed in its regulated operations. An early publication put it this way:

> We will continue our commitment to modernize our Bell Operating Companies and provide equal access to long distance companies. Beyond that, our strategic plan calls for prudent diversification within the information industry. This is the fastest-growing industry in the world, one in which we bring proven expertise to the marketplace. With each new subsidiary, we aim to capitalize on strengths within the organization or opportunities in the marketplace.
>
> We are carefully diversifying into markets that are growing faster and are more profitable than our basic, regulated telephone operations. Since Mountain Bell, Northwestern Bell, and Pacific Northwest Bell are allowed a return on equity ranging up to 16

percent on their intrastate investments, any new venture must show promise to substantially exceed that level.

The company's strategic plan also called for taking advantage of the skills of other companies through mergers, acquisitions, or joint ventures. "Look at the other telephone companies, not the Bell system," said MacAllister, continuing:

> We've been so big that you don't see the trees for the forest. But look at the strategy and structure of United Telephone or Continental. Look, for that matter, at our neighbors to the north—Bell Canada. By my count—and I counted from a chart that is nearly two years old—Bell Canada has ownership positions, ranging from 30 to 100 percent, in eighty-two firms. Eight-two! I admire Bell Canada. It seems to me that they are the current leaders in a strategy that makes a lot of sense.

In 1982 and 1983, managers and strategic planners at U S WEST prepared business plans for six unregulated subsidiaries. In addition to the two specifically allowed by the MFJ—a directory subsidiary (Landmark Publishing, which owned U S WEST Direct) and a customer premises equipment subsidiary (FirsTel Information Systems)—four more were created: (1) NewVector Communications, to manage cellular mobile telephone service; (2) U S WEST Financial Services; (3) Interline Communications Services, a company that engineered, maintained, and managed telecommunications services on consumer premises; and (4) BetaWest, a real estate subsidiary. Interline and FirsTel were joined under the same holding company, U S WEST Services, Inc., early in 1984 (see figure 10–2 for the corporate structure of U S WEST in the spring of 1984).

Nor was U S WEST willing to rest there. In the fall of 1983 MacAllister hired Bob Runice—a marketing executive at AT&T who had begun his career at Northwestern Bell—as president of U S WEST's commercial development division. Runice's charge was to investigate additional opportunities for diversification, perhaps through joint ventures, mergers, or acquisitions.

The operating companies got into the act as well. The three together jointly owned and administered two subsidiary organiza-

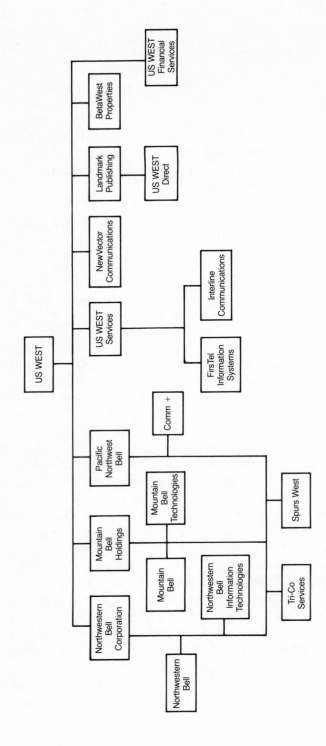

Figure 10–2. *U S WEST Corporate Organization, May 1984*

Source: Courtesy of U S WEST, Inc.

tions—TriCo Services, which provided common staff support, and SpursWest, a purchasing company. In the spring of 1984 Northwestern Bell and Mountain Bell created new holding companies that in turn owned the telephone operating companies and separate subsidiaries to market enhanced telecommunications services (see figure 10–2).

Organization

The organization of U S WEST's corporate headquarters in the spring of 1984 appears in figure 10–3. Reporting to MacAllister as president and CEO were executive vice-presidents DeMuth and Doerr; the vice-presidents of human affairs, public relations, and strategic planning; and the president of commercial development. The presidents of nine subsidiaries also reported to MacAllister.

Many of U S WEST's principles of organization were carried over from Northwestern Bell in the late 1970s, or from the earliest discussions of the regional advisory board. Whatever else the new company would do, it would not attempt to become a smaller version of AT&T. MacAllister explained why:

> AT&T operations and engineering was very directive—they ran the system. They got into the position of writing practices, getting reports, following monthly performance, and so forth. They even had audit teams to see if the operating companies were running according to their standard practices. They had standard phrases for operators. The problem was that they were too far removed from what was happening in the marketplace.

Over time, said MacAllister, U S WEST began thinking of itself not as a telephone company, but as a diversified business that happened to own three telephone companies:

> The Bell System culture had flowed directly out of its mission— and everyone understood it. Our new company would have a different mission that all our people needed to understand and use as a basis for decision making from then on. That mission is simply to enhance our shareholders' investment. But to do so meant

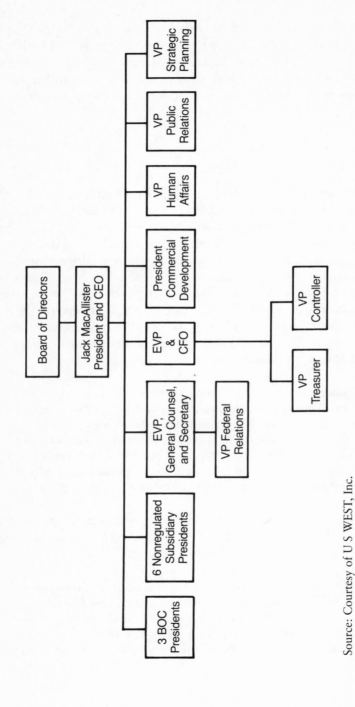

Figure 10–3. *U S WEST Headquarters Organization, May 1984*

Source: Courtesy of U S WEST, Inc.

we would have to conduct ourselves—and our business—very differently.

We decided to organize ourselves as a holding company so we could pursue any opportunity that made sense. We also decided that our three existing companies, and all the ones to follow, would have operating autonomy. U S WEST's staff is not involved in the day-to-day activities of our Bell telephone companies. That means holding company employees concentrate on serving share-owners, while those in the subsidiaries concentrate on serving customers.

Finally, we decided that to compete in a deregulated environment, we would have to deregulate the workplace. And so we made an early decision to limit the number of corporate staff at U S WEST to 100 key managers. We wouldn't have enough people to check, check, and check again. That decision may have been the most significant single action in our effort to change the old culture because it sent a signal, loud and clear, to the entire organization that we weren't going to do things the old way anymore.

The principal mission of the U S WEST corporate staff was to formulate policy and advise the chief executive officer on matters of financial performance, financing and investor relations, business planning and resource allocation decisions, legal issues, financial communications, and personnel management policies. As noted earlier, this was to be done with no more than 100 professional corporate staff managers.

In addition to its basic functions, the staff was expected to "lead by example in the establishment of progressive management style, structure, and the corporate culture changes needed to be more in tune with [its] changing industry." The staff would not involve itself in the day-to-day activities of the BOCs or other subsidiaries, but would work with them in preparing annual business plans and setting general financial goals.

U S WEST made no attempt to impose common organization structures or management systems on its subsidiaries. The organization of the three Bell Operating Companies reflected their different accommodations to AT&T organization directives during the previous ten years and differences in their operating environments and management philosophies. The nonregulated subsidiaries were also free to organize themselves as appropriate to the industries in which they competed. To help the new businesses get started, however, MacAllister gave them internal boards of directors. Each subsidiary president nominated three U S WEST officers to serve on the internal boards, which met monthly to review current operations and future plans. In addition, MacAllister hoped that the inside boards would expose the headquarters staff to practical problems of operating businesses and serve as a training ground to develop general management skills.

Finance and Control

U S WEST's financial goals and policies were partly predicated on the past performance of its three operating companies. On January 1, 1984, U S WEST's total assets stood at nearly $17 billion. According to Howard Doerr, this figure represented a 10.1 percent compound annual growth rate over the previous decade. Net income for the three operating companies averaged increases of 8.5 percent during the previous five years. At the same time, operating expenses had risen about 14.5 percent annually, although, Doerr argued, changes in accounting practices and the tax laws inflated the figure. He also pointed out that the BOCs had made impressive progress in reducing their total payroll. After reaching a high of slightly more than 105,000 employees in 1981, the companies trimmed their work force to 97,400 in 1982, while the divestiture cut the number to roughly 80,000 people.

Nonetheless, Doerr saw the need for U S WEST to continue to control costs and to improve its performance:

> The fourteen-state region composite allowed rate of return on equity is 14.7 percent and you can see that we're a long way from achieving that level. I can assure you that our single most important earnings objective in our regulated business is to earn the allowed rate of return. In addition, we will continue to argue for the 16 percent to 17 percent rate of return that we believe is justified.

A series of decisions by MacAllister, Doerr, and other officers of 1982 and 1983 also helped shape U S WEST's basic financial policies. The underlying thrust was to focus attention on broad measures of financial performance while allowing maximum operating autonomy for the subsidiaries. As Doerr explained the system:

> Our basic financial relationship with the subsidiaries is that we require a 100 percent dividend from them up to the holding company, on a monthly basis. If Northwestern Bell makes $23 million net income in a given month, then $23 million comes to U S WEST as a dividend. Essentially, they give it all to us. In the Bell System, the operating telephone companies used to give up 60 percent to 80 percent of their net income to AT&T; the rest was kept as retained earnings.

In making resource allocation decisions, U S WEST operated like many financial holding companies. The company's organization and policies discouraged headquarters staff from probing deeply into the internal finances of the subsidiaries. The company was especially committed to the operating autonomy of the operating companies. According to Doerr, U S WEST's financial policies represented a very different approach from the one used by AT&T:

> When I was chief financial officer of Northwestern Bell, if we had a $500 million capital program, it had to be approved in every detail by AT&T. Every design and plan had to be approved. Here at U S WEST, we don't even look at them. We get commitments on absolute income and return on investment, and that's all. Our job is to set financial objectives and goals, not to tell the operating companies how to achieve them.
>   We don't question their budget on a line-by-line basis; we just look at the overall picture on the basis of their business plan. If there's not enough capital to go around, we develop a method of allocation based on which subsidiary can earn the highest return on equity.

U S WEST exercised tighter controls over the new nonregulated subsidiaries. The company expected these subsidiaries to earn rates of return comparable with leading competitors in their respective industries. Each subsidiary had a long-range objective of earning 18 to 22 percent. Depending on the maturity of the industry, the subsidiaries had three to seven years to reach these goals. Doerr cited NewVector as an example:

> In cellular radio, we're taking a market-by-market approach. Our first operations are in Denver, Phoenix, Seattle. By late 1985, those markets may be profitable. Then we'll reinvest those profits to enter other markets. We asked NewVector to look at their profitability in each market. We set hurdle rates for new investment, debt structure, and set three- to five-year targets, based on industry standards.

U S WEST took care to keep the boundaries between the BOCs and the nonregulated subsidiaries pure. As Doerr explained:

> Once the dividends from the operating company earnings are passed up to U S WEST, it's the stockholder's money. We may reinvest it in our unregulated subsidiaries, but not at the expense of the ratepayer. By the same token, the operating companies do not guarantee the debt of the unregulated subsidiaries. It is solely an obligation of the subsidiary, which is a separately incorporated entity. This is one reason we can pass the profits of our unregulated subsidiaries straight through to our stockholders, without going through the regulatory process. Since the stockholders put up all the equity and bear all the risk, they are entitled to all the profits.
>
> Of course, we can't take all the money earned by the operating telephone companies and invest it in unregulated businesses. We have to maintain our position in the telephone business, even if it's not currently as profitable as our unregulated businesses will be. For example, if the earnings in Nebraska are bad, we'll still reinvest there, and we won't tell Northwestern Bell to cut spending in Nebraska. They have a franchise to operate, and they have to maintain that franchise. The commitments on income and return on equity at Northwestern Bell were for the region as a whole, not on a state-by-state basis. We at U S WEST are not in the business of redirecting money within the BOCs.

Summing up, Doerr pointed out that "a major effect of divestiture is to put a lot more financial pressure on the BOCs." He admitted some concern about whether the projections made by the subsidiaries were reliable, given U S WEST's decentralized financial policies. "On the other hand," he said,

> we've got a different situation than when we were at AT&T. There, Northwestern Bell was about 3.5 percent of the Bell System; if we missed our target, it didn't have that much impact. Now, Mountain Bell is 50 percent of U S WEST; Northwestern Bell is 28 percent and Pacific Northwest Bell is 22 percent. So we can't afford to have a significant shortfall in any of the operating companies. Even though the operating control is decentralized, we watch things very closely.

Building an Image

Every new company worries about creating and maintaining the right public image, but these concerns were especially urgent at U S WEST. The company was not simply a start-up venture. It also had to contend with strong, entrenched opinions among federal policymakers, the financial community, and the public about the divestiture and the prospects of the BOCs. And it had the further problem of differentiating itself from the other regions. U S WEST officers believed that it was important for securities analysts and regulators to understand the company's distinctive course. Because its strategies of separation, deregulation, and diversification had associated costs and risks, U S WEST was careful to explain why it pursued them.

"The most difficult task we face," said MacAllister, "is trying to demonstrate . . . that we are, in fact, doing things differently. In fact, our new advertising campaign will spell it out very clearly by saying: 'Divestiture created seven new companies. One of them isn't like all the others.'"

U S WEST built its image and its advertising campaign around the region's history and traditions, beginning with the corporate name and logo. As John Felt, vice-president of public relations, described it:

> We wanted to capitalize on our region. It's big, fast-growing, and there's an aura about it. Plus, we didn't want to be seen as just a

regional telephone company. Thus we decided early on to drop the Bell name, except in the operating companies. At the end of 1982, we began working on our image. We interviewed almost every officer in the BOCs and others below that level. The messages we got were, "We want a name that looks to the future, and that capitalizes on who and where we are." From the very beginning, U S WEST was the clear favorite. When the board finally voted on it, early in 1983, the decision was unanimous.

Fallon, McElligot & Rice [an advertising agency] also helped us with the name and to solidify the Western image in our national advertising, which started in the summer of 1983. [See figure 10–4.] We were already writing about wide open opportunity, room to grow, the frontier, and similar themes, but FMR helped us with themes like, "It's impossible to think small in a place this big!" and "We're out to win our spurs!"

The cowboy image is working well. In fact, we're doing very well according to readership and name recognition studies. The financial community rates us first among the regions in effectiveness of advertising and first in effectiveness of investor relations efforts.

Communicating with Investors

It was particularly important for U S WEST to get its message across to securities analysts who would be advising their clients on the value of the divested companies' stocks. In the spring of 1983, as soon as its name was chosen, U S WEST mounted a major effort to reach these analysts. Gary Ames, vice-president and treasurer, joined U S WEST from Pacific Northwest Bell. He described the challenge as follows:

> When I arrived here, we were faced with the fact that within a few months we would start trading on the exchange. We had no name at that point. We were called by at least five different titles in various publications. The first survey we did showed that we had no identity or recognition among the analysts. We knew from the divestiture guidelines that we would start day one with 2.5 million shareowners. Of these, only 4 percent lived in our fourteen states—43 percent of the geographic area of the country. We knew

that our part of the country is not prone to owning blue-chip stocks. We knew that our shareholders were a sleepy audience. The typical shareholder is female, seventy years old, and had inherited stock held for its dividend income. We knew a whole series of things like that, enough to scare the heck out of you.

U S WEST made several important decisions early on. Because it cost roughly $15 to communicate with each shareholder, the company outlined a program to buy back shares and reduce its mailings. It also targeted the twenty most important analysts who were likely to influence opinions on the divestiture. "AT&T tried to stop us from doing this and wanted us to work through their investment bankers," said Ames. "But we said, 'Sharing a lawyer in a divorce doesn't make much sense. It's wonderful that you have these investment bankers, but we don't ever plan on using them.'"

U S WEST initially relied on a national investment bank, but once the company's image and advertising took shape, it managed investor relations on its own. MacAllister, Doerr, Ames, and other officers met with the twenty targeted analysts in New York in April 1983. The company also refined its strategy of advertising. As Ames put it, "We decided not to advertise in anything that was not a financial journal read by those twenty analysts. Of course, another 5,000 analysts who follow telecommunications read the same journals. So we placed our ads in the *Wall Street Journal, Barron's, Business Week,* and other financial journals. We did not put ads in *Time* or *Newsweek* like the other regions did."

Ames also sought out the top fifty institutional owners of stock. He recalled:

My favorite story concerns one of those owners in Los Angeles who, at one point, owned 8 million shares. By default, they would own 800,000 shares of us at the divestiture and if they liked us they could consolidate up to 5.6 million shares. Potentially, I had 6 percent of our stock riding on one contact. So, on the third day of my job, I flew to L.A. without a named employer, a business card, or any of that and spent three and a half hours talking with them about our region and our strategy. People on my staff and I repeated the exercise over and over during 1983.

Source: Courtesy of U S WEST, Inc.

Figure 10–4. *U S WEST Advertisement*

Our 14 state territory is growing faster than any other region created by the divestiture of AT&T. And that includes BellSouth and Southwestern Bell in the much touted sunbelt. U.S. Bureau of Census projections, released in August of this year, confirm it.

Clearly, our region offers unparalleled opportunities for growth.

While this growth will require some capital investment, it will not compromise our ability to perform profitably.

"GO WEST YOUNG MAN."
Horace Greeley, 1851

"GO WEST YOUNG MAN."
John Naisbitt, 1983

Here's why.

Over the last four years our cost to add new customers to the network has been 7% below the Bell System average (1979-1982).

This is because our population is concentrated in urban areas. Our 9 million customers live in less than 40% of the land mass.

Over 90% of our growth is taking place in urban areas, where expansion is most cost efficient. And where our cities are growing 81% faster than the national average. Five of the ten cities of greatest opportunity, cited by John Naisbitt in his book, MEGA-TRENDS, are in our region.

More than half of our new customers will be served by expanding our digital capabilities and applying advanced technology. It is no longer necessary to lay expen-

Our cities are growing 81% faster than the national average. That's why we're the fastest growing region.

sive copper cable to connect every new customer.

During 1983 we are investing $1.7 billion on construction. And all but a fraction of that cost is being financed internally.

We have a strong foundation with more than $15 billion in assets.

U S WEST POPULATION GROWTH WILL OUTPACE OTHER SUNBELT REGIONS FROM 1980 TO 2000.

41% — US WEST
33% — BELLSOUTH
33% — PACIFIC TELESIS GROUP
31% — SOUTHWESTERN BELL

According to a new U.S. Census Bureau Report, August, 1983

Our major subsidiaries will include three established Bell operating companies (Mountain Bell, Northwestern Bell and Pacific Northwest Bell) as well as five new unregulated subsidiaries.

They, too, are poised to profit from our region's growth.

These new companies include INTERLINE (communications management and service), NEW-VECTOR (cellular mobile phone service), U S WEST DIRECT (directory advertising and publishing), a property development and management unit and a subsidiary to market business communications equipment.

It is our intention to be a pacesetter in the fastest growing industry in the world. But we will not stop there.

We will be more than a phone company. With court approval, we can pursue new businesses outside the regulated arena. And, in order to provide the best return to our stockholders, we will.

Before us lies a new frontier, a new beginning and an opportunity to be part of the fastest growing territory on the horizon.

Ask us for more information about U S WEST. Call **1-800-828-2400.** Or write: John Trygg, Director of Investor Relations, U S WEST, 7800 East Orchard Road, Suite 290, Englewood, Colorado 80111.

USWEST

We're out to win our spurs.

Figure 10–4 (*continued*)

U S WEST's advertising was a plus, Ames believed, although he worried that it might be a drawback in some circles:

> Analysts consistently view us as the most aggressive of the seven regions, but the other side of the cowboy image is that some people think it must be lonesome out there on the prairie. "Geez, maybe it's not so hot out there. It must be expensive to wire that," they say. One of the top analysts at Goldman Sachs came out with a report last October that really kind of dinged us. The guy's since become a good friend, but he wrote that our major drawback was our high cost in this territory. I read that, and it really hurt because this guy is very influential. I called him and said, "How do you know our costs are high?" And he said, "Well, they've just got to be." And I said, "Well, how do you know they are?" He said, "Do you know they aren't?" I said, "To be honest, I don't, but I'll call you back." We then did a quick study; it was something we just hadn't done. Hadn't thought about it until somebody was blaming us for it. We found that we were below average on our costs—7 percent below the Bell System. I don't know what that means, but somebody else is higher. We went back to the analyst and demonstrated the findings and he rewrote his report. Unfortunately, the first report had been out there for about a month and it did some damage.

By the summer of 1984 it appeared that U S WEST's efforts were paying off. Of the 20 key analysts the company had identified at the beginning, 15 recommended buying, 3 suggested that owners should hold, and only 2 recommended selling U S WEST stock. According to Ames, no other region came close to that record. At the same time, U S WEST reduced its number of shareholders from 2.5 million to 1.5 million.

Early Returns

In July 1984 U S WEST released its second-quarter review of its financial performance. The company's net income for the first six months totaled $406 million, or $4.23 per share, on revenues of $3.5 billion. This amounted to a 12.7 percent return on investors' equity. U S WEST's dividends for the first two quarters represented about 64 percent of earnings per share. The company also reported its six nonregulated subsidiaries had achieved sales of $72.9 million, or about 4 percent of total revenues during the period.

MacAllister termed these "solid results achieved in a period of unprecedented changes." However, he also argued that revenue performance was hampered by the failure of state and federal regulators to recognize the changing nature of the telecommunications business. He wrote:

> If we're to provide a fully competitive return to investors and maintain our ability to provide universal telephone service, the Federal Communications Commission must come to grips with the important access charge issue. And on the local level, state regulators must allow our companies to price their services to be more competitive.
>
> We think it's time that the government was reminded that divestiture was intended to encourage competition, not to limit it. All we ask is for a fair chance to compete and let customers—not regulators—decide what is in their best interest.

Reenter Judge Greene

In the spring of 1984 U S WEST received its first two waivers from the federal district court allowing the formation of BetaWest, its real estate subsidiary, and approving a joint venture between NewVector and Fluor Corporation to provide cellular phone service to offshore oil rigs in the Gulf of Mexico. In July, however, Judge Greene released his general opinion on the waiver procedure and expressed serious reservations about the diversification strategies of the regional holding companies.

Judge Greene's principal worry was whether the new companies' activities ran contrary to the intent of the MFJ and the broad principles behind it. "No one connected with the negotiation, the drafting, or the modification of the [consent] decree [of 1982]" wrote the judge, "envisioned that the Regional Holding Companies would seek to enter new competitive markets on a broad scale within a few months, let alone a few weeks, after divestiture—before the implementation of equal access and before the companies' commitment to an efficient and economical telephone operation could be tested." Applying an old argument that critics had often directed at AT&T, Greene pointed out that "as long as a Regional Holding Company is engaged in both monopoly and competitive enterprises, it will have the incentive as well as the ability to 'milk' the regulated monopoly affiliate to subsidize its competitive ventures. . . . The more the Regional Holding Companies diversify, the less central their telecommunications functions will obviously become to their corporate existence."

The judge concluded his general remarks by commenting that he did not mean "that the Court will not allow the Regional Holding Companies to engage in other activities, particularly if such activities would tend to increase competition. However," he warned, "if there is to be a 'second phase' restructuring of the telecommunications industry, it will evolve only in a deliberate, cautious manner, with every step tailored to ensure that the public's telephone service does not suffer, but improves in quality and price."

In closing, the judge specified four conditions that the regional holding companies would have to meet for waivers to be approved:[81]

> First, all new businesses must be conducted through separate subsidiaries.
>
> Second, subsidiaries engaged in competitive enterprises must obtain their own debt financing; no entity affiliated with a regional holding company can guarantee this debt in a manner that would permit a creditor to have recourse to the assets of an Operating Company.
>
> Third, the Court will not, for the present, grant waivers for activities whose total net revenues exceed ten percent of the net revenues of the regional holding company's revenues.
>
> Fourth, the regional holding companies must agree to let the Justice Department monitor compliance with the order granting the waiver and report violations.

As he read through the opinion, Jack MacAllister was convinced that U S WEST complied with Judge Greene's conditions and that the company's basic strategy was not threatened. Nonetheless, he wondered whether the opinion would discourage investors and further complicate U S WEST's efforts to communicate its strategy and meet its commitments to shareholders, and whether the 10 percent rule would constrain future opportunities.

Afterword

As we review our chronicle, two principal themes stand out in relief. The first is the technological imperative behind economic change, so powerful as to overwhelm even massive organizations and well-established political interests. The second is the role of leadership and management in presiding over institutional change.

When the Bell system divestiture was announced in January 1982, most analysts hailed AT&T Chairman Charles Brown as a genius. AT&T would retain its dominant position in long-distance communications, its formidable manufacturing capability in Western Electric, and its world-class R&D arm, Bell Labs. The company would at last be freed to compete in the computer business as the 1956 consent decree was vacated. The logic of the settlement implied that AT&T and its competitors in long-distance communications would share the costs of whatever subsidies of local service were required on equal terms. And AT&T would shed the enormous economic burden of completing the transformation of the local loop from copper wire and mechanical switches to electronic and optical technologies. Prospects for AT&T seemed bright indeed.

For the divested operating companies, on the other hand, the future seemed less promising. They would be stuck with a capital-intensive, low-growth utility business and hindered from easy access to the high-tech world of office automation and information management. They would be able to sell customer premises equipment but not to manufacture it. As unregulated equipment manufacturers put more and more switching on customer premises and as bypass technologies continued to emerge, it seemed likely that the operating companies would eventually wither away as the so-called regulated core of telecommunications continued to shrink.

The analysts couldn't have been more wrong—at least from the perspective of 1986. Today's business press tells a very different story from the one outlined four years ago.[1] In 1985 AT&T Information Systems reportedly lost about $900 million and dragged corporate earnings far below the projections of the year before. The company's prospects had deteriorated to that point that a *Wall Street Journal* reporter could write: "After two years in the business, AT&T isn't any further toward challenging IBM in its traditional computer business. . . . In fact, AT&T may never become a computer powerhouse." "More upsetting," the reporter continues, is "a dawning realization" that Chairman Brown

> may have erred when he settled a government antitrust suit . . . by shedding the Bell System's local telephone units to gamble on the faster growing computer industry. The Bell units have turned out to be the shining stars in the eyes of the investment community while AT&T's still-regulated long-distance unit faces increasing competition and while its ability to market computers and phone equipment to business is only marginally improving.[2]

At U S WEST, in contrast, results have been rosy. Performance has improved every quarter since divestiture. In 1985 the company earned more than $900 million on revenues of $7.8 billion. Early in 1986, when the stock was trading in the high 90s, the company's board of directors authorized a two-for-one split and increased its quarterly dividend by 6.3 percent. The company's aggressive management style and award-winning advertising campaigns were drawing national acclaim.[3]

It is tempting to make much of the contrasting performances of AT&T and U S WEST and to attribute these outcomes to differences in leadership and management in the two companies. Clearly these factors have played a role. For example, AT&T's lingering problems appear to be at least partly a legacy of systems and traditions rooted in the past. The headquarters bureaucracy is smaller, but it is still peopled by managers whose expectations and training had prepared them for challenges different from those they now face. Despite the company's considerable assets and still-bright prospects, many AT&T managers look back on divestiture with regret. This focus on the past, on what might have been (or, as many people feel, on what *should* have been), is an obvious hindrance to managing toward the future. Nor has AT&T been able to establish a strong consensus about its mission. Employees in the Bell System knew what the company stood for: service, reliability, and quality as measured by ordinary citizens. In the new AT&T, by all accounts, there are fewer shared values, less agreement around goals, and a much less clear understanding of customers.

At U S WEST, on the other hand, management has evidently succeeded in focusing employees' attention on the challenges of the future. Although the company has not marched forward without an occasional stumble along the way, Jack MacAllister and his top executives have also succeeded in establishing a broad consensus around the strategy of deregulation, competition, and diversification.

The differences between the two companies reflect at least partly different perceptions of the meaning and significance of the changes wrought in the telecommunications industry—and, hence, different responses to these changes. AT&T tended to underestimate and resist the forces driving change; U S WEST, on the other hand, had a clear vision of why change was occurring and sought to embrace it.

Looking back on the chronicle, there is ample reason for contrasting interpretations of the events. Indeed, perhaps the most interesting historical issue is what caused the almost unprecedented restructuring of an entire industry and the breakup of the world's largest corporation over a relatively short period of time. To the public, these developments remain almost nonsensical. Telephone service in the United States was dependable, simple to buy, inexpensive, and reputed to be the best in the world. Why tear apart a system that had worked so well for so long? To business historians and political economists, the problem will be to sort out the causal impact of exogenous factors such as technological change and the broad-based movement toward deregulation in a variety of industries from the structure and behavior of specific institutions and individuals.

The basic engine of change in the telephone industry has been the development of technologies that consistently reduced the competitive advantage of AT&T's integrated network. The concept of a *natural monopoly* used to justify the Bell System's dominance of the telephone industry under price regulation held that the economies of scale or system integration in a single network were so large that they precluded the use of competition as an economic control mechanism. But new technologies changed the underlying costs of the major components of a telephone network. Solid-state electronics reduced the cost of switching; microwave and satellite communications reduced the advantage of owning copper wire. Multiple, competing networks became technologically feasible and economically competitive, first along high-volume corridors and later even where traffic was relatively light. Entry into the long-distance business was made more attractive by the existence of cross-subsidies that artificially raised prices above their competitive level; but given AT&T's high cost structure (a common feature of protected monopolies), competitive entry would have been economically viable even without such distortions.

Given such technological and economic changes, it is not surprising that new companies tried to enter the telecommunications business. What *is* surprising is how futile AT&T's efforts to preserve its regulated monopoly proved to be, despite the corporation's immense political and economic resources and the fragmentation and lack of coordination among institutions such as the FCC, the courts, Congress, and the Justice Department, not to mention AT&T's various business adversaries. One of the enduring images is the spectacle of a huge, powerful, well-financed corporation turning from one public forum to another, losing a legal case here, a regulatory decision there, never able to negotiate with any single party or reach a final, comprehensive settlement of the complex issues involved, until it reluctantly accepted the ultimate solution of breaking up the Bell System.[4] In this regard, the fragmentation of the public policy structure in telecommunications may have been a disadvantage from AT&T's point of view, since it prevented the corporation from focusing its influence on any single agency or institution.

From a public policy perspective, the lack of coordination within the political, judicial, and regulatory structure responsible for telecommunications policy is disturbing, although the ultimate consequences of the breakup of the Bell System are still unknown. The public policy issues in telecommunications are closely inter-related and hence would seem to require a coherent, integrated approach by government. But, as this chronicle makes clear, "gov-ernment" has difficulty developing coherent, integrated policies be-cause it consists of a large number of agencies with overlapping, ambiguously defined roles, viewpoints, responsibilities, and powers. Dramatic decisions like the decision to break up the Bell System may make good legal sense but fail to address crucial technological, economic, or organizational realities, as U S WEST executives ar-gue. Whatever coherence emerges from the disjointed public policy can only be attributed either to an underlying intellectual consensus about key issues such as the value of competition, or to underlying technological and economic forces that drive the whole unwieldy apparatus in more or less the same direction.

Yet, despite the power of such impersonal forces, individuals and institutions do matter. As this chronicle demonstrates, AT&T and U S WEST responded quite differently to changes in the indus-try. AT&T and its executives, especially under John deButts, fought to maintain the Bell System's traditional position as a regulated mo-nopoly and sought to repel new competitors by a variety of legal and—according to the Justice Department—illegal means. Al-though the Bell System adopted new organization structures in 1974 and again in 1978 as part of its response to competition and the need for greater market orientation, there was no change in AT&T's basic strategy, which was still based on the idea of "one system, universal service." Indeed, it would have been almost incon-ceivable for deButts or Brown to maintain a public battle against competition and deregulation and at the same time embrace it as part of AT&T's basic strategy. As a result, AT&T took virtually no effective action to prepare the organization for entry into the com-puter business or for other consequences of reduced regulation and increased competition until the crisis of divestiture was upon it.

On the other hand, Jack MacAllister and top executives at Northwestern Bell and later U S WEST recognized the implications of external trends in technology, deregulation, and competition and took steps to anticipate their consequences. As far back as 1979, MacAllister's "Willing the Future" task force emphasized a forward-looking, almost enthusiastic response to change. Mac-Allister hired external planning consultants, volunteered to experiment with new organizational forms, instituted an employee suggestion program, took an early lead in downsizing the organization, fought to replace mechanistic operating measures of performance with customer satisfaction surveys, and developed new strategic planning approaches, all in an attempt to put his organization in the best possible position to respond to the competitive market and cost pressures he foresaw. And when divestiture came, he threw out AT&T's methods of managing the operating companies in favor of a small corporate staff, decentralized organization, and clear focus on financial performance.

The differences between AT&T and U S WEST can be explained in part by institutional factors. From internal and historical perspectives, AT&T had every reason to fight change and every reason to believe it would win. As a regulated monopoly, AT&T had it all. For all intents and purposes, it *was* the telephone industry; competition could only mean loss of market share, adverse financial consequences from so-called cream skimming by competitors, and increased risk and uncertainty for AT&T's huge bureaucracy. Furthermore, AT&T had been attacked many times in its hundred-year life, and each time had emerged with its monopoly intact. With a reasonably good public image, an immense and geographically dispersed payroll, long experience in government relations, and very deep pockets, AT&T had every conceivable political advantage in its fight against change.

The aggressive strategy adopted by Northwestern Bell cannot be explained solely as a consequence of its position as an operating company, since other operating companies followed AT&T's lead in resisting change. But Northwestern Bell was relatively small and had always been a top performer in the Bell System. Its good performance and small size may have brought it more autonomy from AT&T's general departments than most operating companies enjoyed, and that in turn may have enabled its managers to develop a more flexible style of management than did their peers. As a relatively small operating company, it also had the advantages of being closer to its customers, which may have brought greater awareness of the effects of competition. In any case, Northwestern Bell had a reputation for performance and innovation, and, according to MacAllister, its managers had all been known as mavericks during their careers.

It is clear, however, that MacAllister's character and vision are largely responsible for the forward-looking strategy adopted at Northwestern Bell and later at U S WEST. More than most operating company executives, MacAllister chafed under the constraints of AT&T's massive bureaucracy, its myopic operating measures, and its inflexible management "practices." He sought every opportunity to increase the operating autonomy enjoyed by Northwestern Bell. This desire for autonomy coincided with and was reinforced by the value of a more flexible, decentralized, market-driven style of management under the conditions of increased change, uncertainty, and competitive pressure in the telephone industry. Thus, for MacAllister and like-minded managers at Northwestern Bell and U S WEST, structural change represented more of an opportunity than a threat, in both business and personal terms.

Charles de Gaulle once observed that the essence of statesmanship is to determine the inevitable course of events and then expedite it. Although some might argue that the breakup of the Bell System was hardly inevitable or even necessary, it is clear that regulated monopolies are an anomaly in the U.S. economic system, and have been accepted only where technology creates such large economies of scale or system integration that competition among multiple vendors is not practicable. Where monopolies have been accepted, as in most utilities, rate regulation is used to keep prices and profits as close to competitive levels as possible. The use of the regulatory apparatus to provide cross-subsidies to certain classes of consumers was convenient because it freed legislators from having to use general tax revenues for this purpose, but it was not in itself a sufficient reason for price regulation or for maintenance of a monopoly.

Thus, with the development of electronic switching systems, microwave transmission, and satellite communications, the technological underpinnings of the Bell System's monopoly were destroyed, and hence the monopoly itself became illegitimate and indefensible.

Neither the legal and administrative apparatus of regulation nor the financial and political power of AT&T were sufficient barriers to the entry of new competitors and their exploitation of the Bell System's pricing distortions and high costs. The consequent process of deregulation, cost reduction, and organizational restructuring still continues and, if MacAllister and his colleagues are correct, will not stop until the telecommunications industry is regulated only by competition and the antitrust laws.

Under this view, neither AT&T nor any of the other corporate or public actors involved could have prevented the restructuring of the telecommunications industry, regardless of what their leaders did or failed to do. The leadership challenge was to recognize the inevitable and expedite it. This chronicle suggests that both Brown and MacAllister demonstrated this kind of leadership. Brown's decision to accept the divestiture of the operating companies in return for the retention of AT&T's research, manufacturing, and long-distance units and the opportunity to enter the computer business was indeed an act of leadership, for it marked the acceptance of structural change and a bold move to position AT&T for promising opportunities. Although AT&T has not yet demonstrated an ability to leverage its dominant position in communications into success in the computer business, the basic concept of an integrated communications and computer company still appears sound.

In our view, however, the measure of leadership during a period of change is how early the direction of change is detected and how effectively the process of adaptation is expedited through management action. Critics of AT&T's leadership will argue that deButts and Brown waited too long and did too little to prepare the corporation for its new environment, and that, as a consequence, AT&T may never become the kind of company it might have been. MacAllister's admirers will argue that his excellence as a leader derives from his ability to recognize the need for change before most of his peers, and his willingness to commit himself and his company to action before it was obviously necessary. From the vantage point of 1987, it is unwise to say who is the better leader or which is the better managed company. The problems and the challenges are different; so too will be the correct responses.

Appendix: Executive Changes and New Positions at AT&T, 1982–1984

1982

1/8/82   AT&T agrees to divest itself of twenty-two local operating companies.

1/22/82   William Ellinghaus, president, and James Olson and William Cashel, Jr., vice-chairmen, are removed from day-to-day operations to devote time to corporate strategy, resource allocation, and "other critical issues relating to divestiture."

2/1/82   Charles Marshall named new executive vice-president.

5/10/82   Donald J. Leonard, vice-president–corporate engineering, named vice-president–switching systems at Bell Telephone Laboratories. Succeeds William O. Fleckenstein, who becomes vice-president–operations systems and network planning for Bell Labs.

5/20/82   Seven regional operating company directors named.

6/16/82   Sal Barbera named chief executive officer (CEO), American Bell.

All citations: *Wall Street Journal*, "Who's News" column, and related articles.

8/19/82   Francis J. Heffron elected director of Bell Laboratories, Inc., effective September 1. He will become executive vice-president September 15. Succeeds Harold W. Collier, retiring November 1.

10/18/82   Richard McCormick elected president and CEO of Northwestern Bell. Succeeds Jack MacAllister, who was named chairman of the regional holding company.

10/29/82   Paul M. Villiere, vice-president—network services at AT&T, elected executive vice-president of Western Electric Company.

11/1/82   Morris Tannenbaum named chairman and CEO of interexchange organization. Robert Kleinert, head of Long Lines division, named to additional positions as president and chief operating officer of company's interexchange organization. Sam Willcoxon named executive vice-president—marketing.

11/2/82   Rocco J. Marano elected vice-president.

11/30/82   Irwin Dorros named executive vice-president—technical services. James Hennessy named vice-president—marketing of the Central Services Organization.

12/14/82   Charles Marshall named chairman and CEO of American Bell, Inc. Randall L. Tobias named president of American Bell's consumer products division. Arch McGill named president of the company's new Advanced Information Systems Division.

12/20/82   Alfred C. Partoll, AT&T's vice-president—state regulatory matters, named executive vice-president—external affairs of AT&T's prospective interexchange organization.

12/21/82   Thomas H. Thompson named vice-president—customer products, and Lee S. Tuomenoksa named vice-president—customer services, both for American Bell.

1983

2/14/83 Michael D. Bandhavin named vice-president–government affairs in Washington office of AT&T Central Services Organization.

2/24/83 Salary of AT&T Chairman Charles Brown increased by 17 percent in 1982, while total renumeration—incentive and savings plans, insurance and personal benefits, and contingent renumeration, as well as salary and director's fees—jumps nearly 30 percent to $1.3 million from just over $1 million a year earlier. Salary of William M. Ellinghaus, AT&T's president, rises 9.4 percent in 1982, to $525,000. Mr. Ellinghaus's total renumeration rose 22 percent to $973,359 from $801,023 the year before. In the proxy statement of April 29, AT&T asked shareholders to decrease the par value of its common stock to $1 a share from $16.67 a share to reflect the company's smaller size after divesting itself of its local telephone operating companies.

4/1/83 Michael R. Greene named president and CEO of Advanced Mobile Phone Service Inc.

5/27/83 Robert E. Allen named executive vice-president and CFO of AT&T, succeeding William S. Cashel, Jr., who retires July 1. Cashel had been vice-chairman of AT&T since 1977.

6/7/83 Arch McGill, president of Advanced Information Systems, expected to resign rather than accept a transfer. In separate announcement, AT&T removed operations from American Bell unit to centralize much of its telephone equipment development, manufacturing, and marketing within Western Electric.

6/8/83 McGill resigns as president of American Bell; unit divided into two divisions. Robert J. Casale named division president–marketing and sales of business products and services; Frank S. Vigilante appointed division president–product planning and development.

8/16/83   Randall L. Tobias, president of AT&T Consumer Products, elected a director of Western Electric Company.

8/31/83   Alexander C. Stark, Jr., named president of joint venture with N. V. Philips Gloelampenfabrieken.

9/6/83   Robert D. Dalziel, AT&T assistant vice-president for Bell Operating Company planning and implementation, named vice-president–operations for AT&T International, succeeding Richard E. Pitts, who became vice-president–marketing services for AT&T Communications.

9/21/83   Alfred A. Green, associate general counsel of AT&T, designated vice-president and general counsel for AT&T Communications.

9/27/83   Bruce G. Schwartz, vice-president of business services for AT&T, named division president of AT&T Information Services, effective January 1.

10/5/83   Thomas H. Crowley, executive director of Bell Laboratories' System Software division, named software systems vice-president of Western Electric Co.

10/5/83   Marilyn Laurie, executive director–public relations and employee information, elected vice-president–public relations at Bell Laboratories (subsidiary's first female vice-president).

10/6/83   Kenneth F. Easter, assistant comptroller for Western Electric Company, named vice-president and chief financial officer (CFO) of the parent. Simultaneously appointed vice-president and CFO of Philips Telecommunications B.V., formed by AT&T and N. V. Philips Gloelampenfabrieken of the Netherlands.

10/31/83   Alexander C. Stark, executive vice-president–network operations for AT&T Communications, named president of Philips Telecommunications B. V.

12/9/83	Kenneth J. Whalen, executive vice-president and "an officer with major responsibilities for implementing the divestiture of the Bell System operating companies," retiring at "own request" February 15. Robert E. Allen, executive vice-president and CFO, immediately assumed Whalen's responsibilities for labor relations and personnel. Allen also assumed Whalen's public relations and regulatory matters responsibilities on February 15.
12/13/83	William Ellinghaus to retire in April (AT&T president and chief operating officer).
12/15/83	Western Electric to dissolve; Donald Procknow, Western Electric president, to become vice-chairman of new company.
12/22/83	Five members added to board; Morris Tannenbaum and Charles Marshall join office of chairman.
12/28/83	Michael Sovern and Joseph Williams elected to board.

1984

1/10/84	Victor A. Pelson named executive vice-president of Consumer Products Division, AT&T Technologies Inc. Francis J. Heffron, executive vice-president–staff for Bell Laboratories, succeeds Pelson as executive vice-president–planning and administration at AT&T Technologies.
2/8/84	Raymond E. Williams, director–labor relations, named corporate vice-president–labor relations. Succeeds Rex R. Reed, retiring.
3/29/84	Robert N. Flint to retire as senior vice-president and comptroller, June 30.
3/30/84	Robert M. Kavner, partner in the Coopers & Lybrand accounting firm, named senior vice-president, and CFO as of May 1. Highest AT&T post to be filled from outside since 1980.

4/25/84   William A. Hightower named president of American Transtech subsidiary.

4/30/84   Randall L. Tobias, president of AT&T Consumer Products Unit, named a corporate senior vice-president to assist Chairman Brown on legislative and regulatory matters. Victor A. Pelson named to succeed Tobias as president of AT&T Consumer Products.

7/3/84   John D. Zeglis named executive vice-president and acting general counsel of AT&T Technologies, effective October 1.

8/28/84   Robert J. Casale named to newly created post of executive vice-president of AT&T Information Systems, with responsibilities for financial and strategic planning. The move was noted as "the first of what officials said will be a series of organization changes to strengthen the unit's marketing efforts."

9/12/84   Glenn Watts, CWA president, and Louis Knecht, secretary–treasurer, retire and thereby cut short their union terms "to prepare for complicated bargaining with American Telephone and Telegraph Company."

9/13/84   Thomas J. Berry named to the new post of corporate vice-president–management information and network systems. Frank C. Minter, former corporate vice-president and controller, succeeds Berry as vice-president and CFO of AT&T Information Systems.

11/4/84   Thomas C. Wajnert named president and chief operating officer of new subsidiary, AT&T Credit Corporation.

11/23/84   AT&T names Howard Baker as director, effective January 16.

12/21/84   Lyndell Christensen elected corporate vice-president and secretary for January 1. Additionally responsible for business plans and budgets. Succeeds Thomas Davis, currently retiring, but who maintained responsibilities through February.

12/27/84   Gerald M. Lowrie, chief lobbyist of the American Bankers Association, named AT&T's senior vice-president—public affairs, with responsibilities to oversee the company's dealings with Congress, the White House, and federal departments. Lowrie's appointment marks the second time in 1984 that AT&T went outside the organization to fill a high-level post. Succeeds John G. Fox, who retired in September.

1985

2/1/85   Robert E. Allen appointed chairman of AT&T Information Systems, succeeding Charles Marshall. Marshall appointed executive vice-president for all personnel and external affairs. Randall Tobias named chairman of AT&T Communications. Succeeds Morris Tannenbaum, who takes post as corporate executive vice-president responsible for financial management and strategic planning.

4/3/85   Fox Stoddard named to new post of vice-president—access management at AT&T Communications. Robert Ranalli, vice-president—network, succeeds Stoddard as vice-president—consumer marketing, AT&T Communications.

4/5/85   Daniel H. Wiedemeler named corporate vice-president—human resources. William Ketchum, previously director of marketing services management, succeeds Wiedemeler as division vice-president of AT&T Information Systems.

5/9/85   Roland Pampel named to new post, vice-president—systems marketing and development, for AT&T's computer systems unit.

5/17/85   James Olson named president and chief operating officer. "Likely prospect he will succeed Chairman Brown upon his retirement next year."

6/12/85   Edward Goldstein, corporate vice-president—strategy and development, resigns to join Management Analysis Center in Cambridge, Massachusetts. Goldstein had been with AT&T and the Bell system for thirty-six years.

6/20/85   C. Perry Colwell, formally vice-president and controller of AT&T Technologies, named corporate vice-president and controller of parent.

7/2/85   John E. Berndt, vice-president–market planning at AT&T International, named president and CEO. Succeeds Robert E. Sageman, who retired.

Notes

Preface

1. The series includes five cases under the common heading of *AT&T: Adaptation in Progress* (Harvard Business School Press, 9-481-074 to -077 and -120).
2. Of the cases written since 1980, only *U S WEST, Inc.* (Harvard Business School Press, 9-386-082) and a version of chapter 6 (*AT&T at the Crossroads*, 9-386-089) have been taught in the classroom. These cases are reprinted in a course module edited by Richard H. K. Vietor and Davis Dyer, *Telecommunications in Transition* (Harvard Business School Press, 9-986-001). The other cases (chapters 7 and 9) are published here for the first time.

   Every case in this book save chapter 9 has been reviewed and released by AT&T, Northwestern Bell, or U S WEST. Chapter 9 was written from sources that are publicly available.

Part I: Stability

Chapter 1 is derived from Harvard Business School case 9-481-074, AT&T: Adaptation in Progress (A). Chapter 2 is derived from Harvard Business School cases 9-481-074, AT&T: Adaptation in Progress (A), and 9-481-120, AT&T: Adaptation in Progress (A-1). Copyright © 1981 by the President and Fellows of Harvard College. Used with permission.

1. George David Smith, *The Anatomy of a Business Strategy: Bell, Western Electric, and the Origins of the American Telephone Industry* (Baltimore: Johns Hopkins University Press, 1985), Appendix C, recounts good business reasons for Bell's decision to lease rather than sell.
2. "Deposition of Theodore N. Vail," Circuit Court of the U. S. District of Mass., in equity, *Western Union Telegraph Company et al. v. American Bell Telephone Company* (1899), Record on Exceptions to Master's Report, vol. I, p. 250.
3. United States, Federal Communications Commission, *Investigation of the Telephone Industry in the United States* (Washington, D.C., 1939), p. 150.

4. FCC, *Investigation,* Exhibit 1360A, pp. 206, 217.
5. The Corporations Council of Chicago, quoted in John Brooks, *Telephone: The First Hundred Years* (New York, 1976), p. 114.
6. Robert W. Garnet, *The Telephone Enterprise: The Evolution of the Bell System's Horizontal Structure, 1876—1909* (Baltimore: Johns Hopkins University Press, 1985), esp. chapter 9.
7. Quoted in ibid., p. 173.
8. Ibid., pp. 27–28.
9. Thayer C. Taylor, "AT&T Is on the Line—At Last," *Sales Management,* March 3, 1975, p. 32.
10. American Telephone and Telegraph Company, *Annual Report* (1910), p. 7–8.
11. FCC, *Annual Report* (1974), p. 10.
12. Theodore Newton Vail, *Views on Public Questions: A Collection of Papers and Addresses* . . . (New York, privately published, 1917), p. 13.
13. FCC, *Investigation,* p. 35.
14. "Is That You, Ma Bell?," *Sales Management,* November 11, 1970, p. 19.
15. Quoted in Brooks, *Telephone,* p. 16.
16. FCC, *Investigation,* Exhibit 1360A, p. 169.
17. Quoted in Brooks, *Telephone,* p. 19.
18. This paragraph and the next draw on *Background Note on the Structure of the Telephone Industry* (Harvard Business School Press, 9-680-015).
19. Brooks, *Telephone,* p. 9.
20. William R. Becklean, *The Telecommunications Industry* (New York: Bache Halsey Stuart Shields, Inc., 1979), pp. 19, 26.

Part II: Stress

Chapter 3 is derived from Harvard Business School case 9-481-075, AT&T: Adaptation in Progress (B). Chapters 4 and 5 are derived from Harvard Business School case 9-481-076, AT&T: Adaptation in Progress (C). Copyright © 1981 by the President and Fellows of Harvard College. Used with permission.

1. Bro Uttal, "Selling Is No Longer Mickey Mouse at AT&T," *Fortune,* July 17, 1978, p. 99.
2. "Behind AT&T's Change at the Top," *BusinessWeek,* November 6, 1978, p. 115.
3. Thayer C. Taylor, "AT&T Is on the Line—At Last," *Sales Management,* March 3, 1975, p. 31.
4. "Billed Revenue" was redistributed among various Bell operating units through the separations and settlements process before being entered as "Booked Revenue" in financial statements.
5. Information in this and following sections is based on a report by Jay Galbraith, management consultant to Northwestern Bell.

Part III: Crisis

Chapter 6 is derived from Harvard Business School case 9-386-089, AT&T at Crossroads. Copyright © 1986 by the President and Fellows of Harvard College. Used with permission.

1. Charles L. Brown, "Toward Restructuring: A Perspective on the Shaping of the New Bell System," *Bell Telephone Magazine,* edition 5, 1980, p. 4.
2. Ibid., p. 5.
3. Quoted in the *New York Times,* January 11, 1982.
4. U.S. General Accounting Office, *Legislative and Regulatory Actions Needed to Deal with a Changing Domestic Telecommunications Industry* (Washington, D.C., September 24, 1981), pp. 108, 133.
5. Archie J. McGill, "A New Set of Groundrules," *Datamation,* August 1980, p. 92.
6. Statement of Charles L. Brown on behalf of American Telephone and Telegraph Company, U.S. Senate Committee on Commerce, Science, and Transportation, June 16, 1981.
7. Quoted in R. Z. Manna, "In the Matter of Telecommunications Legislation," *Bell Telephone Magazine,* edition 4, 1981, p. 6.
8. Ibid., p. 9. According to the same article (p. 4), William Baxter, head of the antitrust division in the Justice Department, objected to S. 898 on similar grounds. Baxter believed that the bill lacked precision in providing for network access charges and that it also failed to provide adequate measures to prevent cross-subsidization. See Alvin von Auw, *Heritage and Destiny: Reflections on the Bell System in Transition* (New York: Praeger, 1983), pp. 114–116; Appendix A.
9. Quoted from two speeches by Charles L. Brown: speech to the Armed Forces Communications and Electronics Association, July 1981; and Address to the General Assembly, Telephone Pioneers of America, September 1981.

Part IV: Aftermath

Chapter 10 is derived from Harvard Business School case 9-386-082, U.S. West. Copyright © 1985 by the President and Fellows of Harvard College. Used with permission.

1. Gerald W. Brock, *The Telecommunications Industry: The Dynamics of Industry Structure* (Cambridge, Mass.: Harvard University Press, 1981), p. 15.
2. W. Brooke Tunstall, *Disconnecting Parties: Managing the Bell System Breakup: An Inside View* (New York: McGraw-Hill, 1985), p. 5.
3. Brock, *The Telecommunications Industry,* p. 14.
4. Ibid., pp. 14–15.
5. Adapted from ibid., pp. 300–309.

6. *AT&T News Update,* no. 2, January 11, 1982, p. 4.
7. "Bell System Breakup Opens Era of Great Expectations and Great Concern," *New York Times,* January 1, 1984, p. 12.
8. Adapted from ibid.
9. *AT&T News Update,* no. 1, January 8, 1982, pp. 1–2.
10. *AT&T News Update,* no. 4, January 21, 1983, pp. 1–2.
11. *AT&T News Update,* no. 1, January 8, 1982, pp. 1–2.
12. "Ma Bell's Kids Fight for Position," *Fortune,* June 27, 1983, p. 62.
13. Ibid., p. 64.
14. Ibid., p. 63.
15. Ibid., p. 66.
16. Ibid., p. 67.
17. Ibid., p. 68.
18. "Q&A: Mark S. Fowler. An F.C.C. for the Common Man," *New York Times,* May 25, 1985. Section 3, p. 1.
19. "Congress Seeks to Find If AT&T Breakup Led to Competition or Merely Confusion," *Wall Street Journal,* September 11, 1985, p. 12.
20. Quoted in ibid., p. 12.
21. "Bell System Breakup Opens Era of Great Expectations and Great Concern," p. 12.
22. *AT&T Management Report,* Special Edition, August 27, 1982, pp. 1, 5.
23. *AT&T Management Report,* April 9, 1982, pp. 1–2.
24. *AT&T Management Report,* October 15, 1982, pp. 1–2.
25. *AT&T Management Report,* Special Edition, August 27, 1982, p. 1.
26. Tunstall, *Disconnecting Parties,* p. 133.
27. Ibid., pp. 99, 102.
28. Ibid., pp. 151–152.
29. "Waking Up AT&T: There's Life after Culture Shock," *Fortune,* December 24, 1984, p. 67.
30. Tunstall, *Disconnecting Parties,* pp. 153–154.
31. Ibid.
32. "Waking Up AT&T," p. 70.
33. Ibid.
34. "Struggling to Make the Breakup Work," *New York Times,* July 17, 1983, Section III, p. 27.
35. "Western Electric, 114, Put on Retirement List," *New York Times,* December 15, 1983, Section IV, p. 1.
36. "Can Bell Labs Keep It Up?" *Fortune,* June 27, 1983, p. 90.
37. Ibid.
38. Ibid., p. 91.
39. "Breaking Up the Phone Company," *Fortune,* June 27, 1983, p. 88.
40. "Struggling to Make the Breakup Work," Section III, pp. 1, 27.
41. "Waking Up AT&T," p. 70.
42. "AT&T Seeks Cut of 13,000," *New York Times,* Section IV, p. 1.

43. Ibid.
44. "The Sense of Loss at Ma Bell," *New York Times*, December 28, 1983, Section IV, p. 5.
45. Ibid.
46. Ibid.
47. "Bell Breakup Places Stress on Employees," *Wall Street Journal*, December 30, 1983, p. 11.
48. Ibid.
49. Ibid., p. 25.
50. "Ma Bell and the Hardy Boys," *Across the Board*, July–August 1984, p. 40.
51. "AT&T, in Bid to Lower Costs, Freezes Salaries," *New York Times*, August 5, 1984, p. 1.
52. "AT&T Job Cuts," *New York Times*, August 28, 1984, Section IV, p. 5.
53. "AT&T: Hot Products, High Costs," *New York Times*, August 5, 1984, Section IV, p. 4.
54. Ibid.
55. "AT&T Breakup Plan Is Opposed by Union over Pension Changes," *Wall Street Journal*, February 14, 1983, p. 11.
56. "Bell System's Breakup Is Jarring the Union," *Labor*, May 30, 1983, p. 76.
57. Ibid.
58. Ibid., p. 77.
59. "Phone Message," *Wall Street Journal*, August 23, 1983, p. 32.
60. "Helping Labor and Management Set Up a Quality-of-Worklife Program," *Monthly Labor Review*, U.S. Bureau of Labor Statistics, March 1984, p. 29.
61. Dekkers L. Davidson and Richard H. K. Vietor, "AT&T and the Access Charge," in Richard H. K. Vietor and Davis Dyer, eds., *Telecommunications in Transition: Managing Business and Regulatory Change* Boston: Harvard Business School Press, 1986), pp. 81–112.
62. "AT&T Asks U.S. to Lift Regulations," *New York Times*, April 3, 1984, Section IV, p. 4.
63. "6.1% Cut in Rates on Long Distance Ordered by F.C.C.," *New York Times*, May 11, 1984, Section I, p. 1.
64. Ibid., Section IV, p. 2.
65. "AT&T Seeks Rule Changes," *New York Times*, May 12, 1984, Section I, p. 36.
66. "AT&T Marketing Shift Seen," *New York Times*, June 1, 1984, Section IV, p. 13.
67. "AT&T Gets Union Help," *New York Times*, August 6, 1984, Section IV, p. 2.
68. "AT&T's Ads Get Tougher," *New York Times*, November 28, 1984, Section IV, p. 1.
69. "AT&T Offers Its Computers," *New York Times*, March 28, 1984, Section IV, p. 1.
70. AT&T 1984 Annual Report, *Report of the Chairman*.

71. "Sales Training at the Phone Com . . . Er, AT&T Communications," *Training*, January 1985, p. 66.
72. "Waking Up AT&T," p. 72.
73. "AT&T and the Spinoffs Thrive," *New York Times*, April 25, 1985, Section IV, p. 1.
74. *Communications Week*, April 8, 1985, pp. 1, 39.
75. *Wall Street Journal*, May 9, 1985, p. 5.
76. Alvin von Auw, *Heritage and Destiny* (New York: Praeger, 1983), p. 58.
77. "IBM Agrees to Acquire 16% Holding in MCI: Alliance Would Create Powerful Challenge to AT&T," *Wall Street Journal*, June 27, 1985, p. 3.
78. *United States of America* v. *Western Electric Company, Incorporated, and American Telephone and Telegraph Company*, Civil Action No. 82-0192, *Modification of Final Judgment*, U.S. District Court for the District of Columbia, August 24, 1982, pp. 6–7.
79. Although the company's name was not chosen until February 1983, for convenience's sake it is hereafter referred to as U S WEST.
80. *Modification of Final Judgment*, pp. 1–2.
81. *United States of America* v. *American Telephone and Telegraph Company, et al.*, U.S. District Court for the District of Columbia, July 26, 1984. (Quotations taken from Judge Harold H. Greene's *Opinion*, pp. 22, 9, 32, and 44, respectively. Conditions summarized from pp. 53–56.)

Afterword

1. Janet Guyon, "The Progress of AT&T in the Computer Business Proves Disappointing," *Wall Street Journal*, May 12, 1986, pp. 1, 19; "Why AT&T Isn't Clicking," *BusinessWeek*, May 19, 1986, pp. 88–95.
2. Guyon, "The Progress of AT&T," p. 1.
3. E.g., "The Baby Bells Take Giant Steps," *BusinessWeek*, December 2, 1985.
4. Nor, as subsequent events have shown, did the breakup of the Bell System create a final solution to the problems of technological change, regulation, and competition, which still face AT&T.

Glossary

BMS Bell Marketing System, an interrelated set of marketing concepts, job designs, and organizational structures developed in the mid-1970s. Modeled on IBM's approach to marketing.

BOCs Bell Operating Companies.

Centrex A central exchange service provided to large customers. Replaces switching of telephone lines at Bell central offices.

Common carrier An entity that transmits communications for the general public at accepted rates.

CI-II Computer Inquiry II. FCC decision in 1980 allowing AT&T to enter competitive markets in customer premises equipment and enhanced services through a separate subsidiary.

Enhanced services Communications services that integrate transmission and information processing.

FCC Federal Communications Commission.

Interconnect Normally refers to the connection of non-Bell customer premises equipment to the Bell telephone network.

LATAs Local access and transport areas. As part of the 1982 consent decree, the United States is divided into roughly 160 LATAs (corresponding to the U.S. Census Bureau's Standard Metropolitan Statistical Areas). As of January 1, 1984, the BOCs are generally restricted to providing in-

---

The glossary is derived from material appearing in Richard H. K. Vietor and Davis Dyer, eds., *Telecommunications in Transition: Managing Business and Regulatory Change* (Boston: Harvard Business School Press, 1986), pp. iii, 219–221.

tra-LATA telephone service, whereas AT&T handles most intercity and inter-LATA service.

Local exchange   Telephone switching service provided for a specific local area, such as part of a city.

Long-distance exchange   Connects locations beyond range of local exchange.

MFJ   Modification of Final Judgment. Judge Harold H. Greene's final terms for divestiture of the Bell System, August 1982.

PBX   Private branch exchange. Customer premises equipment that allows customers to switch telephone lines on own premises rather than at the telephone company's central office.

PUC   State public utility commission.

SCCs   Specialized common carriers, term used to describe interstate common carriers other than traditional telephone companies.

Separations and settlements   Traditional accounting procedures in Bell System that classifies telephone property as intra- or interstate and returns revenues from interstate services to subsidize local exchange services.

Switch   Device that connects two or more telephone lines for the duration of a call.

Index

About the Authors

Leonard A. Schlesinger is executive vice president and director of Au Bon Pain Co., Inc., a rapidly growing chain of French bakery/cafes and wholesale manufacturer of frozen dough products for supermarkets and food service institutions, headquartered in Boston, Massachusetts. Prior to joining Au Bon Pain, he served as associate professor of business administration at the Harvard Business School, where he taught and did research in organizational behavior and human resource management. Dr. Schlesinger has consulted on large-scale organizational change projects throughout North America and Mexico, most notably with Cummins Engine, Honeywell, Citibank, First National Bank of Chicago, and Ciba-Geigy. He holds a bachelor's degree from Brown University, a master's in corporate and labor relations from Columbia University, and a doctorate in organizational behavior from Harvard University.

Davis Dyer is director of The Winthrop Group, a firm headquartered in Cambridge, Massachusetts, that specializes in historically based consulting for business and government. He also teaches a course in business history at Harvard University Extension. He was formerly an associate editor of the *Harvard Business Review,* a senior research associate at the Harvard Business School, and an assistant professor of management at Boston College. He has A.B., A.M., and Ph.D. degrees in history from Harvard University.

Thomas N. Clough is a consultant with Cambridge Associates, Inc., in Boston. He formerly taught at Harvard and Boston Universities. He holds a bachelor's degree from Harvard College and a doctorate in business administration from the Harvard Business School.

Diane Landau is an international market planner for developing countries at AT&T Network Systems. Prior to working at AT&T she was a consultant and a project manager/assistant to the director of Latin American/Asian Affairs at Volunteers In Technical Assistance, and she worked on a government and business project at McCall Publishing Company. She has a bachelor of science degree from Northwestern University and a master of public administration degree from Harvard University.